Is Religion Killing Us?

Is Religion Killing Us?

Violence in the Bible and the Quran

JACK NELSON-PALLMEYER

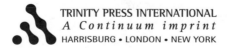

TRINITY PRESS INTERNATIONAL
A Continuum imprint
HARRISBURG • LONDON • NEW YORK

Trinity Press International, P.O. Box 1321, Harrisburg, PA 17105
Trinity Press International is a division of The Morehouse Group.

Cover photo: Portrait of Young Girl Looking Sad, photograph by Mel Curtis, PhotoDisc.
Cover design: Trude Brummer

Library of Congress Cataloging-in-Publication Data

Nelson-Pallmeyer, Jack.
    Is religion killing us? / Jack Nelson-Pallmeyer.
        p. cm.
    Includes bibliographical references and index.
    ISBN 1-56338-408-6
    1. Violence in the Bible. 2. Violence in the Koran. 3. God—
Wrath—History of doctrines. 4. Violence—Religious aspects—
History of doctrines.   I. Title.
    BS680.V4N45 2003
    291.5'697—dc21

2002012930

Printed in the United States of America

03 04 05 06 07 08   10 9 8 7 6 5 4 3 2 1

To
THICH NHAT HANH

Contents

Acknowledgments

I WOULD LIKE TO THANK Henry Carrigan at Trinity Press International, who offered enthusiastic support for this book; my wife Sara and children (Hannah, Audrey, and Naomi) who bring joy to my life and accept my early morning writing sprees; my students and colleagues in Justice and Peace Studies at the University of St. Thomas who take faith, nonviolence, and peacemaking seriously; and Matt Smith and Dave Gagne who offered support and helpful suggestions throughout.

Introduction:
The Elephant in the Room

I WAS TAUGHT THAT RELIGION WAS GOOD, necessary, and at the heart of life because it dealt with issues of ultimate consequence and meaning. Much later I learned that what made religion good and necessary also made it prone to intolerance and violence. Religion kills, or more accurately, religion is used to justify killing precisely because issues of ultimate consequence and meaning are understood to be at stake. People rarely kill each other for reasons of religious difference alone. They do frequently use God and religion, however, to justify killing when conflicts escalate between individuals, groups, or nations. In the midst of problems rooted in land, oppression, discrimination, or any number of other historical grievances, religion is often called on to justify human violence with subtle or not so subtle reference to "sacred" texts, divine mission, or moral purpose.[1]

There were many things I didn't know about religion when I was instructed in the Christian faith. I was busy with baseball and bicycles and found religion relatively benign, though something of a nuisance as my brothers and I tried in vain not to squirm or giggle during services. As a teen, I experienced the church as a place of deep friendships and bewildering theology. During confirmation classes, I occasionally asked questions outside the box. I wondered why a loving God would drown nearly all of humanity, why God allowed earthquakes, and why a baby who died before being baptized went to hell. Musings like these met a stern response from a pastor who essentially told me to shut up and memorize the truths found in the Bible and the tradition.

As a college student involved in protesting the U.S. wars in Indochina, I wondered why my church, including most parishioners, gave uncritical support to the U.S. war effort. Friends and I who were former leaders of our youth group were shunned when we suggested that saturation bombing, defoliation, napalm, cluster bombs, maimed civilians, destroyed villages, and elevated body counts were hard to reconcile with Jesus, who blessed peacemakers and taught love of enemies. One angry parishioner told me that if I objected to war, I shouldn't be a Christian. To bolster his case, he challenged me to read the Bible. He said—accurately, as I learned many years later—that it was filled with stories in which a violent God approved of war.

My Christian formation did not include information about other religions. It dawned on me later that my pastors and teachers believed that *only* the Christian religion was right about God, and it alone conveyed the true meaning of life and faith. I was taught that the Bible was holy because it was "God's Word" and that belief in Christ was the only way to God because Jesus said so. I was required to memorize the creed and selected Bible verses. I was told never to doubt. At the time I didn't know how much horrific violence was attributed to God in the Bible or that other religions, including Islam, had "sacred" or "holy" texts in which God's dominant character was said to be compassionate but was equally steeped in violence.

I had never considered that exclusive claims to Truth at the heart of the monotheistic religions made violent conflict likely if not inevitable. It was only within the last decade, many years after receiving a Master of Divinity degree, that I read the Bible and the Quran cover to cover. I confess that the unrelenting violence-of-God traditions I encountered when reading these "sacred" texts in their entirety made atheism for the first time seem a credible option (one I reject).

Although the problem of religion and violence extends well beyond the conduct and "sacred" texts of Jews, Christians, and Muslims, I focus attention in the pages that follow primarily on the violence-of-God traditions within the Bible and the Quran. Violence, of course, is not the only story line in these texts, or people wouldn't turn to them for guidance. The Hebrew Scriptures express love for God and neighbor, advocate for widows and orphans, call forth justice, promote debt forgiveness, and in a variety of ways encourage ethical behavior. The Christian New Testament affirms many of these impulses. It encourages service, gives voice to the poor, blesses peacemakers, and promotes social justice. Although the lesson is ignored by many Christians, Jesus teaches love of enemies and exposes the futility of violence. The Quran also places a strong emphasis on social justice and ethical behavior. It rejects infanticide, prohibits adultery, defends orphans, advocates for the poor, and with words nearly identical to Hebrew scriptural counterparts, encourages just measures and right balances in the marketplace.

I accept that there are positive streams within the Bible and Quran. The problem that has been ignored for too long, however, is that these streams flow from and are flooded by an enormous reservoir of God's abusive violence. Despicable portraits of a violent, seemingly pathological God and of murderous human conduct justified in relation to the divine overwhelm hopeful and insightful passages. As sociologist and peace educator Elise Boulding notes, "The warrior god has dominated the stories of our faith communities, so that the other story, the story of human caring and compassion and reconciliation, is often difficult to hear."[2]

In a world fracturing because of violence, much of it sanctioned by religion, we must honestly face the problem of violence and "sacred" texts. Judaism, Christianity, and Islam, rooted in parallel and yet conflicting texts, make competing claims about God and history. *Each "sacred" text is dominated by violence-of-God traditions.* Violence-legitimating texts do not lead automatically to human violence. They do, however, make violence more likely in the midst of conflicts in which antagonistic parties count religious differences among issues that divide them.

Human violence is inevitable so long as those of us who are practitioners of competing faiths give legitimacy to violence-of-God traditions. We memorize texts understood as sacred, receive instructions not to doubt, and believe that our religion or particular interpretation of our faith tradition is the true and perhaps only expression of God's will in an unjust world. It is sobering to realize that we live in a world brought to the brink of destruction by religious and political certitude, and yet both the Bible and the Quran discourage doubt, giving warnings backed up by threats of violent punishments.

Violence-of-God traditions are the heart of the Bible and the Quran. This is the elephant in the room of which nobody speaks. Through some combination of lectionary gymnastics[3] and claims of divine or divinely inspired authorship, believers give authority to texts that are directly or indirectly killing us. We avoid talking about the elephant in the room for a variety of reasons. As a Christian, I have a legitimate desire not to offend the religious sensibilities of Jews, Christians, and Muslims. I also am aware that many believers are afraid that if aspects of our "sacred" texts are challenged, we may be left without a firm foundation for faith.

Is Religion Killing Us? speaks honestly about the elephant in the room. It presents evidence that portrayals of God as punishing and violent and of God's power as coercive and abusive are the *dominant themes* in these "sacred" texts. If religion is going to help us respond creatively to a world torn apart by injustice and engulfed in a spiral of violence,[4] then we must take an honest look at the violence-of-God traditions at the heart of the "sacred" texts of Judaism, Christianity, and Islam.

My fundamental claim is that *religiously justified violence is first and foremost a problem of "sacred" texts and not a problem of misinterpretation* of the texts. The problem, in other words, is not primarily that people take passages out of context and twist them in order to justify violence. The problem is actual violence at the heart of these texts that can be reasonably cited by people to justify their own recourse to violence.

Ignoring an elephant in a room, not surprisingly, has rather grave consequences. *Is Religion Killing Us?* therefore addresses four sub-themes related to the violence-of-God traditions at the heart of the Bible and the Quran. First, it describes how acceptance of violence-of-God traditions within "sacred" texts encourages human violence and sanctions abusive notions of power. The dominant images of God's power in the Bible and the Quran reinforce an understanding of power as power over others. Effective power, both divine and human, is expressed in terms of fear, rewards and punishments, defeat of enemies, and superior violence. It should give us pause that men dominate ruling circles and religious institutions within a world that is being destroyed by inequality, violence, and war; that women are generally second- or third-class citizens; and that war, violence, and women's oppression are often reinforced by claims of divine will rooted in "sacred" texts written and dominated by men.

A second subtheme in *Is Religion Killing Us?* is how the widespread acceptance of violence-of-God traditions solidifies the relationship between violence and the divine so completely that functionally violence is the *real religion in the world today*. Most people—including believers, atheists, Christians, Muslims, Marxists, Jews, politicians, clergy, revolutionaries, counterrevolutionaries, communists, capital-ists, anarchists, fundamentalists, government leaders who sanction state-sponsored terror, and terrorists who fly airplanes into trade cen-ters—believe that violence saves. If religion and faith are about ulti-mate allegiance, then it can be said that violence is the world's principal religion.

A third subtheme in *Is Religion Killing Us?* is the particular crisis of Christianity, violence, and "sacred" texts in the context of U.S. mil-itarization. The problem of Islam and violence was raised in the after-math of the terrorist attacks on the World Trade Center and the Pentagon of September 11, 2001, but hardly anyone has broached the subject of Christianity and violence in the context of a militarized U.S. foreign policy that preceded and followed the terrible violence of that day. The seriousness of this oversight is brought into focus when we consider that the United States is far and away the world leader in war spending, weapons sales, and military violence; that 84 percent of U.S. adults identify themselves as Christian;[5] and that the nonviolence of Jesus is featured prominently within the "sacred" text of Christianity but is ignored by all but a few Christians.

Finally, *Is Religion Killing Us?* seeks a way out of the spiral of violence at the heart of the world's life. It presents ideas for alternative ways to approach "sacred" texts so that we can learn from both their distortions and their insights concerning God and faith. It argues that our well-being depends on our willingness to doubt aspects of both our religious traditions and our political worldviews, and that the quality of our future depends on our capacity to see the world through the lens and experiences of our enemies.

Many human beings, myself included, understand ourselves as spiritual creatures. We search for meaning in life in a religious context. We struggle to make sense out of our lives, historical events, beauty, setbacks, pain, and joy—all in relation to the divine. Our spiritual journeys throughout life are shaped by our experiences, our socialization, the tradition handed down to us (what others taught us to believe), the "sacred" texts that we hear and interpret and consult, and the lives of past and present practitioners of faith from family members to prophets. I still assent to the claim that religion is good, necessary, and at the heart of life because it deals with issues of ultimate consequence and meaning. I do so, however, only in the context of an honest assessment of the destructive role violence-of-God traditions within "sacred" texts play in a world fractured by violence, inequality, war, intolerance, and hate. Treating texts rooted in the violence-of-God traditions in the Bible and the Quran as "sacred" distorts God and faith and gives religious legitimacy to human violence. Challenging those traditions and texts is an essential act of faithfulness for believers in the twenty-first century.

NOTES

1. I often put quotation marks around "sacred" because designating the Bible and the Quran as sacred generally gives legitimacy to, or leads to uncritical acceptance of, the violence-of-God traditions at the heart of these texts. The issue of what authority we should give to these texts will be a central theme throughout this book.

2. Elise Boulding, *Cultures of Peace: The Hidden Side of History* (Syracuse: Syracuse University Press, 2000), 11.

3. By lectionary gymnastics I mean the common practice of skipping verses (or entire passages) during biblical readings for Sunday church services in order to avoid the full weight of God's pathological violence present in both the Hebrew Scriptures and Christian New Testament. For example, the assigned Old Testament reading for Sunday, June 2, 2002, was Deuteronomy 11:18-21, 26-28. Read the missing verses (22-25) for a classic example of lectionary gymnastics.

4. The spiral of violence is a concept that emerged out of Latin American liberation theology. It refers to a vicious circle in which oppression gives rise to rebellion, and then rebellion gives rise to repression, in a never-ending and mutually reinforcing pattern. I will adapt and address the spiral of violence in chapter 2.

5. "Faith in America," by Jeffrey L. Sheler, *U.S. News & World Report,* May 6, 2002, 43.

1. Lunatics and Messengers

Our encouragement and call to Muslims to enter Jihad against the American and the Israeli occupiers are actions which we are engaging in as religious obligations. Allah Most High has commanded us in many verses of the Quran to fight in His path and to urge the believers to do so. Of these are His words: "Fight in the path of Allah, you are not charged with the responsibility except for yourself, and urge the believers, lest Allah restrain the might of the rejectors, and Allah is stronger in might and stronger in inflicting punishment." . . . We have given an oath to Allah to continue in the struggle as long as we have blood pumping in our veins or a seeing eye, and we beg of Allah to accept and to grant a good ending for us and for all the Muslims.

    —Osama bin Laden[1]

As long as the United States of America is determined and strong, this will not be an age of terror. This will be an age of liberty here and across the world. . . . Our nation, this generation, will lift the dark threat of violence from our people and our future. We will rally the world to this cause by our efforts, by our courage. We will not tire, we will not falter, and we will not fail. . . . The course of this conflict is not known, yet its outcome is certain. Freedom and fear, justice and cruelty, have always been at war, and we know that God is not neutral between them. Fellow citizens, we'll meet violence with patient justice, assured of the rightness of our cause and confident of the victories to come. In all that lies before us, may God grant us wisdom, and may He watch over the United States of America.

　　—President George W. Bush[2]

---ᴜ⌐---

NOT LONG INTO THE TWENTIETH CENTURY, Samuel Clemens (Mark Twain) wrote "The War Prayer." His daughter told him not to print it because it would be regarded as sacrilege. A friend inquired, "Still, you are going to publish it, are you not?" "No," Clemens said, "I have told the whole truth in that, and only dead men can tell the truth in this world. It can be published after I am dead." Twain's words spoken from the grave were a commentary on religion and war and more specifically on Christianity and war in the context of the United States at the time of World War I.

"The War Prayer" describes "a time of great and exalting excitement." "The country was up in arms, the war was on, in every breast burned the fire of patriotism." Young volunteers marched while "proud fathers and mothers and sisters and sweethearts" cheered them on "with voices choked with happy emotion." The people listened "to patriot oratory which stirred the deepest deeps of their hearts," while "in the churches the pastors preached devotion to flag and country and invoked the God of Battles, beseeching His aid in our good cause."

Sunday, the day before a new wave of soldiers was to depart for the front, "the church was filled," "a war chapter from the Old Testament was read," and a long prayer was uttered.

None could remember the like of it for passionate pleading and moving and beautiful language. The burden of its supplication was that an ever-merciful and benignant Father of us all would watch over our noble young soldiers and aid, comfort, and encourage them in their patriotic work; bless them, shield them in the day of battle and the hour of peril, bear them in His mighty hand, make them strong and confident, invincible in the bloody onset; help them to crush the foe, grant to them and to their flag and country imperishable honor and glory. Bless our arms, grant us the victory, O Lord our God, Father and Protector of our land and flag!

At this point an "aged stranger" stepped into the scene, noticed by the parishioners but not by the pastor, who "with shut lids" continued "his moving prayer." The stranger introduced himself as having "come from the Throne—bearing a message from Almighty God!" God, he told the baffled parishioners, "has heard the prayer of His servant your shepherd and will grant it if such shall be your desire after I, His messenger, shall have explained its import—that is to say, its full import." Full import comes from considering the implications of the prayer for those on the other side of the battlefield. "If you would beseech a blessing upon yourself, beware lest without intent you invoke a curse upon a neighbor at the same time," he cautioned. "You have heard your servant's prayer—the uttered part of it," the messenger continued. "I am commissioned of God to put into words the other part of it—that part which the pastor, and also you in your hearts, fervently prayed silently. And ignorantly and unthinkingly? God grant that it was so."

The unwanted messenger of God told those gathered that their spoken and unspoken prayer would have dire consequences that they themselves perhaps did not intend. "You heard these words," he reminds them. " 'Grant us the victory, O Lord our God!' That is sufficient. The whole of the uttered prayer is compact into those pregnant words." Those words have "many unmentioned results which follow victory." The messenger's task was to put the unspoken part of the prayer into words:

> O Lord our Father, our young patriots, idols of our hearts, go forth to battle—be Thou near them! With them, in spirit, we also go forth from the sweet peace of our beloved firesides to smite the foe. O Lord our God, help us to tear their soldiers to bloody shreds with our shells; help us to cover their smiling fields with the pale forms of their patriot dead; help us to drown the thunder of the guns with the shrieks of their wounded, writhing in pain; help us to lay waste their humble homes with a hurricane of fire; help us to wring the hearts of their unoffending widows with unavailing grief; help us to turn them out roofless with their children to wander unfriended the wastes of their desolated land in rags and hunger and thirst, sports of the sun flames of summer and the icy winds of winter, broken in spirit, worn with travail, imploring Thee for the refuge of the grave and denied it—for our sakes who adore Thee, Lord, blast their hopes, blight their lives, protract their bitter pilgrimage, make heavy their steps, water their way with their tears, stain the white snow with the blood of their wounded feet! We ask it, in the spirit of love, of Him Who is the Source of Love, and Who is the ever-faithful refuge and friend of all that are sore beset and seek His aid with humble and contrite hearts. Amen.

The prayer had been spoken and heard and would be granted if the people still wanted their petitions fulfilled after understanding the full accounting of their meaning. "If ye still desire it, speak!" "The

War Prayer" ends with chilling words: "It was believed afterward that the man was a lunatic, because there was no sense in what he said."[3]

GOD ON OUR SIDE

The lunatic looked like a prophet at century's end. "The tragedy of the twentieth century," Elise Boulding writes, "is that it began with the promise of bringing an end to war as an instrument of state diplomacy but is ending as the world's bloodiest century, with 108 million war dead."[4] The tragedy of the twenty-first century may be our failure to learn anything from the previous one.

The sentiments of "The War Prayer" are no less sacrilegious and no less dangerous in our post-September 11th world in which Twain's "aged messenger" would likely still receive a lunatic's reception. People often frame political and economic conflicts and their responses to them in religious terms, out of conviction and/or to justify their actions. Those who benefit from existing systems explain their good fortune in relation to divine gifts, and justify violence in defense of their privileges by citing the depravity of their enemies and God's will to keep them at bay. Those who are marginalized by existing systems often view present injustices as a result of oppression, foreign domination, God's punishment for infidelity, or a strange combination of each. In any case, punishing those responsible for the injustices and fighting for greater justice are understood to be essential acts of faithfulness. People often resort to violence in seeking redress, claim God's blessing in doing so, or call on God to bless or supplement their own violence with divine power.

We see many of these dynamics at play in the terrorist attacks of September 11, 2001, and in the U.S. response to those attacks. These events mark a bloody and violent beginning to a new century, with the last century having shifted warfare in the direction of greater and greater lethal violence, in which civilian casualties predominated. God, predictably, is understood to be the benefactor of each side in the deadly conflict, as the quotes from Osama bin Laden and President Bush that introduced this chapter make clear. The Muslims who flew airplanes into the World Trade Towers and the Pentagon did so in service to Allah. They understood themselves to be instruments of God's will, agents of deserved punishments, and bearers of divine justice against enemies sufficiently evil so as to do away with the category of innocent civilians. Terrorist actions were for them a *faithful response to historical grievances based on a faithful reading of their sacred text.* As Osama bin Laden said in a February 1998 interview:

> Praise be to God, who revealed the Book, controls the clouds, defeats factionalism, and says in His Book, "But when the forbidden months are past, then fight and slay the pagans wherever ye find them, seize them, beleaguer them, and lie wait for them in every stratagem (of war)"; and peace be upon our Prophet, Muhammad Bin-'Abdallah, who said, I have been sent with the sword between my hands to ensure that no one but God is worshipped, God who put my livelihood under the shadow of my spear and who inflicts humiliation and scorn on those who disobey my orders. The Arabian Peninsula has never—since God made it flat, created its desert, and encircled it with seas—been stormed by any forces like the crusader armies spreading in it like locusts, eating its riches and wiping out its plantations. All this is happening at a time in which nations are attacking Muslims like people fighting over a plate of food. . . . All these crimes and sins committed by the Americans are a clear declaration of war on God, his messenger, and Muslims. And ulema [mullahs, religious leaders] have throughout Islamic history unanimously agreed that the jihad is an individual duty if the enemy destroys the Muslim countries. . . . Nothing is more sacred than belief except repulsing an enemy who is attacking religion and life. On that basis, and in compliance with God's order, we issue the following fatwa [religious legal opinion] to all Muslims: The ruling to kill the Americans and their allies—civilian and military—is an individual duty for every Muslim who can do it in any country in which it is possible to do it, in order to liberate the al-Aqsa Mosque and

the holy mosque [Mecca] from their grip, and in order for their armies to move out of all the lands of Islam, defeated and unable to threaten any Muslim. This is in accordance with the words of Almighty God, "And fight the pagans all together as they fight you all together," and "Fight them until there is no more tumult of oppression, and there prevail justice and faith in God."[5]

As will become clear in chapter 6, the preponderance of violent images of God in the Quran make it difficult to argue that Osama bin Laden is distorting the text in order to justify his actions. He is citing passages from the Quran and applying them to present historical crises. His theology and his actions, in other words, are reasonable in light of the "sacred" text he studies and cites. Muslims are under attack. Islam is under attack. Oppression must be resisted. Violent resistance is not only justified in the Quran; it is also a requirement of faith.

This troubling pattern of grievance followed by violent response justified in relation to faith, God, or sacred text is also evident in the U.S. response to the terrorist attacks. U.S. leaders peppered their pronouncements of retaliatory actions—including the relentless bombing of Afghanistan and broader war against terrorism—with references to God. The rhetoric of President Bush and his advisers post-September 11 is eerily similar to that of Osama bin Laden and his supporters. Each side poses the conflict as a struggle between good and evil. In response to the depth of evil to be countered, each justifies the death of civilians, whether targeted (bin Laden) or as collateral damage (U.S. leaders). Each believes the grave depravity of the other can only be countered with lethal violence. Each invokes God's name to ground the righteousness of their cause.

People in the United States and throughout much of the world were rightfully outraged at Osama bin Laden's clearly stated presumption that terrorist attacks against the United States were faithful actions reflecting Allah's will. Not noticed by most U.S. citizens but equally offensive to many people worldwide is the unspoken assumption of many U.S. leaders and citizens that the United States and its military are God's chosen instruments to establish justice in a world of profound injustice and evil. Post-September 11 sentiments echoed those of U.S Senator Albert J. Beveridge in a speech he delivered in 1898:

> God has . . . made us the master organizers of the world to establish system where chaos reigns. He has given us the spirit of progress to overwhelm the forces of reaction throughout the earth. He has made us adept in government that we may administer government among savage and senile peoples. Were it not for such a force as this, the world would relapse into barbarism and night. And of all our race He has marked the American people as His chosen nation to finally lead in the regeneration of the world. This is the divine mission of America, and it holds for us all the profit, all the glory, all the happiness possible to man. . . . What shall history say of us? Shall it say that we renounced that holy trust, left the savage to his base condition, the wilderness to the reign of waste, deserted duty, abandoned glory? No! They founded no paralytic government, incapable of the simplest acts of administration. . . . They unfurled no retreating flag. That flag has never paused in its onward march. Who dares halt it now—now, when history's largest events are carrying it forward.[6]

Religious rhetoric often masks self-interest. As Beveridge himself said, the goals of the U.S. were not primarily noble or altruistic. "American factories are making more than the American people can use. American soil is producing more than they can consume. Fate has written our policy for us; the trade of the world must and shall be ours. . . . We will cover the ocean with our merchant marine. We will build a navy to the measure of our greatness."[7] In a similar way, religious rhetoric, spoken and received with self-evident confidence by most U.S. citizens following September 11, including Christians, obscured from view oil interests, civilian casualties, decades of disastrous U.S. foreign policy initiatives in the Middle East, and the U.S. role in training Islamic fundamentalist extremists and other terrorists for its own purposes in many parts of the world.

The problem of selective vision masking deep contradictions in U.S. policy was the subject of George Monbiot's article "Backyard Terrorism" published in the London-based newspaper *The Guardian* just over a month and a half after the attacks of September 11. President Bush had warned that "if any government sponsors the outlaws and killers of innocents, they have become outlaws and murderers themselves" and "will take that lonely path at their own peril." Monbiot responded:

> I'm glad he said "any government," as there's one which, though it has yet to be identified as a sponsor of terrorism, requires his urgent attention. For the past 55 years it has been running a terrorist training camp, whose victims massively outnumber the people killed by the attack on New York, the embassy bombings and the other atrocities laid, rightly or wrongly, at al-Qaida's door.

Monbiot links terrorism to the U.S. government and to a U.S. military training school with roots in Panama and presently located in Fort Benning, Georgia. He details numerous atrocities linked to the U.S. Army School of the Americas (recently renamed the Western Hemisphere Institute for Security Cooperation) and contends that U.S. government leaders refuse to acknowledge the school's horrific human rights record or to close it down even though "the evidence linking the school to continuing atrocities in Latin America is rather stronger than the evidence linking the al-Qaida training camps to the attack on New York."[8]

The above examples demonstrate a number of important issues. First, a terrorist may be a freedom fighter in someone else's eyes. Both Osama bin Laden and U.S. leaders have used terrorist tactics in pursuit of political objectives. Second, making sense out of the world by dividing it into separate camps of good and evil is a prescription for perpetual violence and ultimate disaster. There is, of course, no justification for turning airplanes into instruments of terror. There are, however, reasons why people do so. When we dismiss these reasons as the irrational charges of evil and crazed lunatics who attack us because of our goodness, we do so to our own and the world's peril. The fact that Osama bin Laden is guilty of massive crimes against humanity and is thus wrong to orchestrate terrorist attacks against civilians in the name of Allah does not necessarily mean that his criticisms of the United States are without merit. That is why, as John Esposito writes in *Unholy War: Terror in the Name of Islam,* many of bin Laden's criticisms of the United States and the West resonate with the "perceptions and grievances of mainstream as well as extremist Muslims."[9]

Finally, in the above examples we see the troubling picture of violence being linked to God, faith, and religion by all parties in any given conflict. In a world being destroyed by violence, much of it with religious overtones, we need to take an honest look at the problem of religion, violence, and "sacred" text. Those who justify lethal violence against enemies, including the religious other, can and do find inspiration in their sacred texts that are dominated by violent images of God and by stories that legitimate human violence in service to God's will. Parties in any given conflict can call upon competing "sacred" texts or competing passages within the same "sacred" text to justify violence, hatred, and war. They can do so because matters of ultimate consequence and meaning are said to be at stake in their conflict with the other, and because *the "sacred" texts to which they turn are filled with images of a violent God/gods and with stories and passages that legitimate human violence against the other in service to God's will.* Not surprisingly, "divine will," in both text and their mind's desire, frequently conforms to their own wishes and desires for conquest, revenge, land, resources, justice, revolution, counterrevolution, or power.

NOTES

1. Emergency Net NEWS Service, 1998, online, http://www.emergency.com/bladen98.html.

2. Associated Press, "Bush Speech: Transcript" (Sept. 20, 2001).

3. Mark Twain, *The War Prayer* (New York: Harper & Row, 1971).

4. Elise Boulding, *Cultures of Peace: The Hidden Side of History* (Syracuse, N.Y.: Syracuse University Press, 2000), 233.

5. Emergency Net NEWS Service, 1998.

6. John M. Blum et al., *The National Experience: A History of the United States* (New York: Harcourt Brace Jovanovich, 1963), 533.

7. Ibid.

8. George Monbiot, "Backyard Terrorism," *The Guardian* (Oct. 30, 2001). I have written two books on the School of the Americas. For the most recent one, see Jack Nelson-Pallmeyer, *School of Assassins: Guns, Greed, and Globalization* (Maryknoll, N.Y.: Orbis Books, 2001).

9. John L. Esposito, *Unholy War: Terror in the Name of Islam* (New York: Oxford University Press, 2002), 22.

2. Religion and Violence

For you don't count the dead with God on our side.
   —Bob Dylan

—⊐∟—

SEPTEMBER 11 BROUGHT THE ISSUE OF GOD and violence into focus, albeit through a distorted lens. The spotlight was on Islam because Muslim extremists had flown airplanes into the World Trade Towers and Pentagon in the name of Allah. Within days, however, it should have been clear that the focus on Islam, God, and violence was too narrow: Christian fundamentalist T.V. evangelists interpreted the terrorist attacks as deserved punishments from God. "The Rev. Jerry Falwell and Pat Robertson set off a minor explosion of their own," Laurie Goodstein reported in the *New York Times,* "when they asserted on television on Thursday [two days after the attack] that an angry God had allowed the terrorists to succeed in their deadly mission because the United States had become a nation of abortion, homosexuality, secular schools and courts, and the American Civil

Liberties Union. . . . Mr. Falwell's and Mr. Robertson's remarks," she wrote, "were based in theology familiar to and accepted by many conservative evangelical Christians, who believe the Bible teaches that God withdraws protection from nations that violate his will." Goldstein reported the exchange between Falwell and Robertson:

> What Mr. Falwell said Thursday on "The 700 Club," while chatting with the program's host, Mr. Robertson, was this: "What we saw on Tuesday, as terrible as it is, could be minuscule if, in fact, God continues to lift the curtain and allow the enemies of America to give us probably what we deserve." Mr. Robertson responded, "Jerry, that's my feeling. I think we've just seen the antechamber to terror. We haven't even begun to see what they can do to the major population." A few minutes later Mr. Falwell said, "The abortionists have got to bear some burden for this because God will not be mocked. And when we destroy 40 million little innocent babies, we make God mad. I really believe that the pagans, and the abortionists, and the feminists, and the gays and the lesbians who are actively trying to make that an alternative lifestyle, the A.C.L.U., People for the American Way, all of them who have tried to secularize America, I point the finger in their face and say, 'You helped this happen.' " To which Mr. Robertson said, "Well, I totally concur, and the problem is we have adopted that agenda at the highest levels of government." Mr. Robertson also issued a press release on Thursday saying that in a country rampant with materialism, Internet pornography, and lack of prayer, "God almighty is lifting his protection from us."[1]

CONFUSING MESSAGES

One could hardly blame God for being confused by all the competing rhetoric and demands in the pre- and post–September 11 period. Leading up to the attacks, Osama bin Laden called on Allah to help Muslims respond to an unprecedented threat. What "bears no doubt in this fierce Judeo-Christian campaign against the Muslim world, the likes of which has never been seen before," he said, "is that Muslims must prepare all the possible might to repel the enemy on the military, economic, missionary, and all other areas." He asked "Allah to give" the Muslim community "the guidance to exalt the people who obey Him and humiliate those who disobey Him, and to give us a rule where decency is commanded and evil is forbidden."[2] Following the attacks and especially after the U.S.-led military campaign began in Afghanistan, U.S. citizens, including many Christians, placed "God Bless America" posters, flags, and decals in every conceivable locale. Bible sales soared, as did church attendance. Many religious leaders gave their blessings to the U.S. war against terror, saying that it conformed to Just War principles. President Bush said confidently that God is not neutral in conflicts such as these, implying that God is with us in our noble cause of hunting down terrorists. The president also noted how "all of America was touched on the evening of the tragedy to see Republicans and Democrats joined together on the steps of this Capitol singing 'God Bless America.' "[3] Meanwhile, Jerry Falwell and Pat Robertson declared God to be the architect of the terrorist attacks. God was "lifting his protection from us" because of the sins of feminists, abortionists, homosexuals and civil libertarians. Where, we might ask, is Twain's "aged messenger" today?

RELIGIOUS WAR?

Despite God talk from many sides in the conflict, the post-September 11 focus remained on Islam. Was Islam inherently violent? Were the actions of Osama bin Laden and other Islamic terrorists consistent with the Quran and representative of Islam? Commentators, religious leaders, and politicians, including President Bush—after using "crusade" to describe the U.S. commitment to fight terrorism— were careful to disassociate Islam from terrorism. He and others stressed repeatedly and rightly that the actions of Muslim extremists should not distort views of mainstream Islam or become the occasion for scapegoating violence. "The terrorists practice a fringe form of

Islamic extremism that has been rejected by Muslim scholars and the vast majority of Muslim clerics; a fringe movement that perverts the peaceful teachings of Islam," President Bush told the nation a few days after the attack.

> I also want to speak tonight directly to Muslims throughout the world. We respect your faith. It's practiced freely by many millions of Americans and by millions more in countries that America counts as friends. Its teachings are good and peaceful, and those who commit evil in the name of Allah blaspheme the name of Allah. The terrorists are traitors to their own faith, trying, in effect, to hijack Islam itself. The enemy of America is not our many Muslim friends. It is not our many Arab friends. Our enemy is a radical network of terrorists and every government that supports them.[4]

It is, of course, important not to paint all Muslims with the broad strokes of terrorism based on the actions of extremists, just as it would be unfair to see all Christians through the lens of Jerry Falwell's Christianity. It would also be wrong to single out Islam as if to suggest that the problem of God, religion, and violence is unique to Muslims or the Quran. It is, however, a serious mistake to downplay the problem of religion, violence, and "sacred" text in its many forms. As I will demonstrate in the next several chapters, Jews, Christians, and Muslims who look to the Bible or the Quran for guidance find hundreds and hundreds of passages that rightfully can be called upon to bolster their claims that violence and hatred against enemies are not only justified but reflect the will of God.

Andrew Sullivan, in an article "This *Is* a Religious War" in *The New York Times Magazine,* writes that the "general reluctance" to speak about "the conflict that began on Sept. 11" as a religious war is "admirable" but wrong. "The only problem with this otherwise laudable effort is that it doesn't hold up under inspection. The religious dimension of this conflict is central to its meaning. The words of Osama bin Laden," Sullivan writes, "are saturated with religious argument and theological language. . . . The terrorists' strain of Islam is clearly not shared by most Muslims. . . . But it surely represents a part of Islam—a radical, fundamentalist part—that simply cannot be ignored or denied."

This "surely is a religious war," Sullivan continues, yet it is not a war between Islam, Christianity, and Judaism but rather "a war of fundamentalism against faiths of all kinds that are at peace with freedom and modernity." Sullivan states clearly that the "use of religion for extreme repression, and even terror, is not restricted to Islam. For most of its history," he says, "Christianity has had a worse record." The Crusades, Inquisition, and bloody religious wars during the sixteenth and seventeenth centuries meant that "Europe saw far more blood spilled for religion's sake than the Muslim world did." He continues:

> It seems almost as if there is something inherent in religious monotheism that lends itself to this kind of terrorist temptation. And our bland attempts to ignore this—to speak of this violence as if it did not have religious roots—is some kind of denial. We don't want to denigrate religion as such, and so we deny that religion is at the heart of this. But we would understand this conflict better, perhaps, if we first acknowledged that religion is responsible in some way, and then figure out how and why.[5]

Martin Marty wrote a thoughtful post-September 11 article titled "Is Religion the Problem?" in the progressive Jewish publication *Tikkun*. Marty, who has spent years studying religious fundamentalism, offers numerous examples of religiously justified violence. The "killing dimension of religion is an interfaith phenomenon," he writes. "It's not only something that 'they' do, or something in 'their' scriptures. Nor is the lethal side of religion a monopoly of monotheists, the peoples of the Book, as a quick look at religions of the world will reveal."

"Hindu extremists, using the *Bhagavad Gita* as a sacred script," Marty writes, used these words in their fight against the British: "Take up arms and protect religion. When one is face to face [with the enemy,] they should be slaughtered without hesitation. Not the slightest blame attaches to the slayer." In the name of Kali the Hindu goddess, "lay down your life but first take a life. . . . The worship of the goddess will not be consummated if you sacrifice your lives at the shrine of independence without shedding blood."

"Are Eastern religions peaceful?" Marty asks. It is a rhetorical question aimed at Westerners who sometimes assume so. "Yet Theravada Buddhist monks in Sri Lanka," Marty writes, "long active in Sinhalese affairs, have been at war with Tamil Hindu separatists since 1983." One well-known monk "urged 'Young Buddhists of Asia' to 'Arise, awake, unite and join the Army of Holiness and Peace and defeat the hosts of Evil.' They did." Marty quotes another scholar who says that although Japanese Buddhism "has never declared a holy war," it "has nonetheless proclaimed all Japanese wars holy." And as Marty himself says, the "religious atrocity of devotees of Shinto, which inspired Japanese militarism through World War II, is too notorious to be overlooked."

"As for Sikhism," Marty writes that "followers of Jarmail Singh Bhindranwale, a Punjabi maverick preacher, believe their enemies 'are perpetrating atrocities on us, . . . burning our Holy Book. . . . There is no need to get a license for arms.'" Bhindranwale told his followers to "prepare for war" and that the concept of peaceful means "cannot be found together in any part of the Sikh scriptures, in the history of the Gurus, nor in the history of the Sikhs." As for Jews, Christians, and Muslims, Marty writes:

Monotheists . . . have no monopoly on violence. But it is true that scripturally revealed monotheism can serve those minded to be lethal in distinctive ways. Believe in one all-powerful God. Believe that this God has enemies. Believe that you are charged to serve the purposes of God against those enemies. Believe that a unique and absolute holy book gives you directions, impulses, and motivations to prosecute war. You have, then, the formula

for crusades, holy wars, jihads, and, as we relearned in the year
just passing, terrorism that knows no boundaries.

Thus, in Allah's name, some Muslim fundamentalists have
fought other Muslims, and, as everyone knows and in ways that
need no further documentation at year's end, non-Muslims.
The Muslim fundamentalists' enemies in Israel, Jews in movements such as Gush Emunim ("Bloc of the Faithful"), have in
turn cited the Torah to define boundaries of their Israel and to
inspire militant policies and actions. They don't need Muslims
to point out the many Bible stories, such as those in the Books
of Joshua and Judges, that tell of divinely sanctioned war for
ancient Israel and were used for battle in the birth of mainly
secular modern Israel.

As for Christians, the Muslims, especially Arabs, retain a
fresh memory of the Crusades, the blood-shedding disasters
that, beginning in 1095, rallied troops with the cry "God wills
it." . . . Christians have used Christianity to justify slavery of
Africans and the removal to reservations, or death, of Native
Americans. In the American Civil War, the North acted with
God's "terrible swift sword," and the Southern cause came to
be "baptized in blood." Afterward, Protestants in the Ku Klux
Klan employed chaplains, read Bibles, and mounted crosses as
they set out against blacks, Catholics, and Jews.[6]

Marty deserves praise for being among the few commentators
willing to raise the problem of God, violence, and "sacred" text. Sullivan too broaches this subject in relation to the Quran. "Most inter-
preters of the Quran find no arguments in it for the murder of
innocents," he writes.

But it would be naïve to ignore in Islam a deep thread of intolerance toward unbelievers, especially if those unbelievers are
believed to be a threat to the Islamic world. There are many
passages in the Quran urging mercy toward others, tolerance,

respect for life, and so on. But there are also passages as violent
as this:"And when the sacred months are passed, kill those who
join other gods with God wherever ye shall find them; and seize
them, besiege them, and lay wait for them with every kind of
ambush."[7]

The vast majority of Muslims reject terrorism, but it is also true
that the Muslims who flew airplanes into the World Trade Towers and
the Pentagon on September 11 could have cited many passages from
the Quran as motivation for their terrorist actions, which were for
them a faithful response to Allah. It is equally sad that similar passages
and related violence-of-God traditions lie at the heart of the "sacred"
texts and unholy actions of Christians and Jews. Religious violence is
first and foremost a problem of "sacred" text, not misinterpretation of
"sacred" text. The violence-of-God traditions in the Hebrew Scriptures, the Christian New Testament, and the Quran must be understood and challenged if we are to have any realistic hope of building a
peaceful world.

THE VIOLENCE OF GOD AND THE SPIRAL OF VIOLENCE

The next several chapters document how violence-of-God traditions
are embedded in the heart of the Bible and the Quran. Chapters 3–4
examine the violence-of-God traditions in the Hebrew Scriptures.
Chapter 5 looks at how these traditions carry over into the Christian
New Testament, including how violent expectations of God's actions
frame and distort interpretations of the meaning of Jesus' life and
death. Chapter 6 explores the violence-of-God traditions in the
Quran. To set the stage for these reflections, I close the present chapter with a brief description of liberation theology's concept of a *spiral
of violence,* a comprehensive understanding of violence that is central
to my arguments in the chapters that follow.

Latin American liberation theology emerged in the 1960s in
response to social systems in which the misery of hungry majorities
contrasted sharply with the lifestyles and power of the opulent few.

Liberation theology stresses God's desire and human responsibility to work for justice. It affirms the dignity of the human person and the need for political and economic priorities and systems to reflect and foster dignified living. It says that God sides with the oppressed in struggles for justice, and therefore people and institutions of faith must exercise a preferential option for the poor. Liberation theology roots sin in both individual conduct and in the structures of society. In its Christian form, it understands the crucifixion of Jesus to be a consequence of Jesus' faith, which led him to confront oppressive groups and institutions in first-century Palestine; it affirms the resurrection as validation of Jesus' life, which Christians are to emulate.

Liberation theology was considered dangerous by the U.S. government and its powerful political, economic, and religious allies in the region. People who lived out their faith in light of liberation themes and commitments were brutally repressed.[8] Ironically, in the context of violence against followers of liberation theology, critics accused that theology of fomenting violence. Liberation theologians responded by articulating a comprehensive view of violence known as the spiral of violence. It has three key dimensions or spokes: violence 1, 2, and 3.[9] Violence 1 is characterized by oppression, hunger, and poverty. Children who die of hunger or who are stunted by malnutrition are victims of violence. So too are people whose ill health, illiteracy, and death are linked to economic inequalities or concentrated land-ownership, whatever directly or indirectly prevents them from receiving medical care, attending school, or receiving adequate nourishment. This expansive definition links violence to social injustice and moves beyond traditional meanings that focus too narrowly on guns and warfare. Liberation theology speaks of institutionalized violence and social sin in order to highlight that violence 1 is rooted in the structures of unjust societies.

Violence 2, the second spoke in the spiral, is characterized by rebellion. People living in poverty or misery or in the midst of other oppressive situations sometimes strike out violently against those they hold responsible for their misery. Violence 2 is a response to and predictable outcome of violence 1. People who protest against violence

1 often do so nonviolently. They demonstrate, petition, unionize, strike, vote, and boycott. Peaceful protests, however, are often met with repressive violence (violence 3); the apparent absence of redress through nonviolent means can lead to rebellion (violence 2) that is often the result of desperation and not design. It is considered an option of "last resort."

Violence 3, according to liberation theology, is the repressive violence used by elite forces against those who protest or rebel. This includes the lethal violence of military forces aligned with the state and with foreign or domestic economic elites, and the terror and torture practices of paramilitary groups and death squads associated with them. Most rebellions are violently suppressed because the resources and lethal violence of the state and its allies are generally far superior to that of protesters and insurgents. State violence and terror (violence 3) can successfully, though sometimes only temporarily, crush violent rebellions (violence 2), but in doing so they often deepen the violence of hunger, poverty, oppression, and social inequality (violence 1). Since the causes of injustice remain, there are new protests, some violent, followed by more repression as the spiral of violence intensifies.

The spiral of violence profoundly challenges people of faith. Religion often bolsters the power of economic elites and sanctions the repression of the state. Liberation streams within Judaism, Christianity, and Islam insist that structural injustices be addressed. This means participation in actions that address violence 1 in an effort to overcome the systemic causes of hunger, poverty, and oppression. It also requires an honest assessment of whether theology, dogma, and "sacred" text encourage liberation or injustice, and whether they encourage violent or nonviolent means in pursuit of justice. At the same time, religious institutions and individual believers must sever their political ties to elites and discredit the repressive violence of the state (violence 3) that reinforces unjust systems (violence 1).

As I examine the violence-of-God traditions in the "sacred" texts of Jews, Christians, and Muslims, I do so in the context of a spiral of violence with five rather than three spokes. To oppression (violence 1), rebellion (2), and repression (3), I add the categories of dysfunctional deflective violence (4) and spiritual violence/violent images of God (5). Dysfunctional deflective violence (4) is violence used against others that doesn't challenge unjust systems. Violence in the context of rebellion is often understood as a necessary means to bring about greater social justice. Dysfunctional deflective violence, by way of contrast, is rarely motivated by justice or linked to political goals. It often involves poor people striking out at other poor people because they are nearby and not because they are understood to be power brokers in an unjust system. Dysfunctional deflective violence increases as poverty and exclusion feed despair and as communities break down. A contemporary example would be the high incidence of murder and crime that characterizes many impoverished neighborhoods.

Dysfunctional deflective violence shifts people's anger away from individuals or institutions that exercise power within unjust systems and onto others. It leaves powerful systems in place and powerful people unnamed. It thrives in an environment in which people internalize the worldview of the oppressive system. Dysfunctional deflective violence makes life miserable for many and feeds a spiral of community hostility and breakdown. Much violence in the world today, in my view, is encompassed in violence 4.

By spiritual violence (5), I mean images of God that explain human misery as God's will or project human desire for vengeance onto God within or at the end of history. Many violent portraits of God and actions attributed to God by the writers of "sacred" texts reflect spiritual violence. God uses floods and she-bears to punish. God commands followers to engage in holy war in defense of religion or territory. God delivers battlefield victories. God reduces disobedient people to cannibalism as punishment for sin. God's credentials are established through superior violence. God promises to crush the people's enemies directly or enable "the people of God" to do so. Contemporary examples of spiritual violence include explanations that Hurricane Mitch, the terrorist attacks at the World Trade Towers, and AIDS are God's response to sin. They also involve threats of hell and damnation used to condition behavior, and any and all efforts to justify human violence and holy warfare through appeals to the divine.

SPIRAL OF VIOLENCE

Violence 1	Violence 2	Violence 3	Violence 4	Violence 5
Hunger, Poverty, Oppression	Rebellion, Armed Resistance, Fighting Back	Repression, State Terror, Death Squads, Military Oppression	Dysfunctional- Deflective, Community Breakdown, Crime	Spiritual, Divine Threats, Awaiting God's Violence, Human Violence in God's Name

The violence-of-God traditions within the "sacred" texts of Jews, Christians, and Muslims intersect with the spiral of violence in conflicting and disturbing ways. It is to those traditions and "sacred" texts that I now turn.

NOTES

1. Laurie Goodstein, "After the Attacks: Finding Fault; Falwell's Finger-Pointing Inappropriate, Bush Says," *New York Times* (Sept. 15, 2001).

2. "Mujahid Usamah Bin Ladin Talks Exclusively to *Nida'ul Islam* about the New Powder Keg in the Middle East," Nida'ul Islam (online, http://www.islam.org.au), issue 15 (Oct. 1996), online, http://www.islam.org.au/articles/15/LADIN.htm.

3. Associated Press, "Bush Speech: Transcript" (Sept. 20, 2001).

4. Ibid.

5. Andrew Sullivan, "This *Is* a Religious War," *The New York Times Magazine* (Oct. 7, 2001): 45–46.

6. Martin E. Marty, "Is Religion the Problem?" *Tikkun* (Mar./Apr. 2002).

7. Sullivan, "This *Is* a Religious War," 45.

8. See Jack Nelson-Pallmeyer, *School of Assassins: Guns, Greed and Globalization* (Maryknoll, N.Y.: Orbis Books, 2001).

9. Helder Camara, *Spiral of Violence* (London: Sheed & Ward, 1971).

3. Violence-of-God Traditions in the Hebrew Scriptures

Has any god ever attempted to go and take a nation for himself from the midst of another nation, by trials, by signs and wonders, by war, by a mighty hand and an outstretched arm, and by terrifying displays of power, as the LORD your God did for you in Egypt before your very eyes? To you it was shown so that you would acknowledge that the LORD is God; there is no other besides him. (Deut 4:34–35)[1]

See, the day of the LORD comes,
   cruel, with wrath and fierce anger,
to make the earth a desolation,
   and to destroy its sinners from it. . . .
Whoever is found will be thrust through,
   and whoever is caught will fall by the sword.
Their infants will be dashed to pieces before their eyes;

their houses will be plundered,
and their wives ravished.
See, I am stirring up the Medes against them. (Isa 13:9, 15–17a)

───⏑⏛───

THE VIOLENCE-OF-GOD TRADITIONS that lie at the heart of the "sacred" texts of Jews, Christians, and Muslims are rooted in images of God featured centrally in the Hebrew Bible. Taking cues from the Hebrew Scriptures, Jews, Christians, and Muslims are monotheists (believers in one God). They are considered to be "peoples of the Book," and they agree that God is one, powerful, and firmly in control of human history. The Bible and the Quran speak of God as compassionate and merciful, but they depict God's power in overwhelmingly male terms, that is, as violent, coercive, punishing, threatening, and deadly.[2]

MONOTHEISM AND VIOLENCE

The Hebrew Scriptures reflect speculations about God over a period encompassing nearly two thousand years of human history. The many priestly writers who contributed to these texts drew on oral and written traditions about many different gods with a wide array of names, characteristics, and functions. Rather late in the Jewish tradition, priestly writers imposed a monotheistic outlook (belief in one God) on materials that for many centuries had reflected life and faith in a polytheistic setting (belief in many gods).

As Judaism's one-God tradition took shape, it embraced a powerful deity. As I described in *Jesus Against Christianity,* Yahweh absorbed powers associated previously with other gods:

It took many centuries for Judaism's one God to emerge as a powerful, composite deity with many characteristics of neighboring gods and religions. As Jewish monotheism evolved and took shape, there was no longer a need for a human fertility goddess such as Anat because Yahweh opened and closed wombs and promised more children than the stars to those who were chosen and faithful. If your worship of God or the gods was prompted by concern or gratitude for agricultural abundance, then you need not worship Baal because Yahweh was at the head of the council of gods and Yahweh was the one who delivered or withheld harvests. If you worshiped wind or thunder, then you might find an acceptable alternative in Yahweh, who created and controlled these and other powerful forces of nature. If you longed for divine intimacy and therefore worshiped El or other personal Gods of Egypt or Canaan, then Yahweh could be your God. Just as El wrestled with Jacob and told the patriarchs where to go and whom to marry, Yahweh walked with Adam and Eve in the garden, made them clothes, grieved over their sin, and involved himself in daily life and human history. If, on the other hand, divine intimacy offended your religious sensibilities because it made God seem too close or too human-like, then you need not dismiss or abandon Yahweh worship because there were priests who grafted opposite characteristics onto Yahweh, including Elohim's cosmic otherness and transcendence. If you needed a militarily powerful God, were awed and led to worship God because of violence, or understood God as superior violence, then you could reject Tiamat, Marduk, and Baal. Yahweh's violence was impressively displayed through genocidal floods, plagues, and military triumphs. Yahweh's violence was powerful, operated within history, and could be appropriated by the faithful against their enemies. Much later in the tradition, under Persian influence, faith was linked to life after death. You need not worship Ahura Mazda, however, because Yahweh held the keys to both life and life after death.[3]

These ideas and views were those of late priestly writers, but they would not have been widely shared by people in Israel throughout much of biblical history. As priestly writers forced monotheistic assumptions on both people and "sacred" text, God's power, priestly power, and human violence done in God's name increased dramatically. Violence increased because the one, powerful God was understood to be a jealous God. God gave blessings to a select group and required followers to destroy the religious icons of other gods and/or their religious devotees.

> When the LORD your God brings you into the land that you are about to enter and occupy, and he clears away many nations before you. . . , seven nations mightier and more numerous than you—and when the LORD your God gives them over to you and you defeat them, then you must utterly destroy them. Make no covenant with them and show them no mercy. . . . But this is how you must deal with them: break down their altars, smash their pillars, hew down their sacred poles, and burn their idols with fire. For you are a people holy to the LORD your God; the LORD your God has chosen you out of all the peoples on earth to be his people, his treasured possession. (Deut 7:1–2, 5–6)

God was also understood to punish disobedience. The power of priests was rooted in their claim to know what pleased or displeased an almighty, jealous Deity. They also controlled the redemptive mechanisms through which those who had offended the Deity could return to favor. The Hebrew Bible, as I explained in *Jesus Against Christianity*, presents abundant evidence that conflicting priestly groups lifted up competing and incompatible descriptions of God, including different names, characteristics, worship sites, and other requirements:

> Some priests said you could sacrifice to Yahweh only in Jerusalem. Others disagreed. Some said when you sacrificed to Yahweh outside of Jerusalem you were really sacrificing to El. Others disagreed. Some sacrificed directly and openly to El. Others thought doing so prompted God's punishing violence. Some spoke of Yahweh as close and personal. Others said Yahweh was

distant. Some said Yahweh was merciful. Others understood Elohim, who underwent a name change (Yahweh), to be without mercy. Some spoke about Levites and priests as the same thing. Others said Levites were subordinate to priests linked to Aaron. Others denied the legitimacy of priests tied to Aaron and asserted that ties to Moses were necessary for divine approval. These conflicts led to violence and fed the pathology of God as adversaries claimed divine approval.[4]

The stakes in such disputes were very high:

If anyone secretly entices you—even if it is your brother, your father's son or your mother's son, or your own son or daughter, or the wife you embrace, or your most intimate friend—saying, "Let us go worship other gods," whom neither you nor your ancestors have known, any of the gods of the peoples that are around you, whether near you or far away from you, from one end of the earth to the other, you must not yield to or heed any such persons. Show them no pity or compassion and do not shield them. But you shall surely kill them; your own hand shall be first against them to execute them, and afterwards the hand of all the people. Stone them to death for trying to turn you away from the LORD your God, who brought you out of the land of Egypt, out of the house of slavery. Then all Israel shall hear and be afraid, and never again do any such wickedness. (Deut 13:6–11)

Believers like to think of "sacred" texts as God's words, or at least as words inspired by God, but elite priestly writers were often guided by self-interest. They reinforced their own power by writing their privileges into the "sacred" text. As Richard Horsley argues, The " 'Priestly writers' of early postexilic times [when the Hebrew Scriptures were compiled and edited] reconstructed and virtually established a religious tradition as a way of legitimating the 'restored' Jewish social-political order."[5]

Violent images of God that took root in, and in many ways took over, the Hebrew Scriptures impacted the faith traditions of Jews, Christians, and Muslims; such images set the stage for potential deadly conflict. The Hebrew Bible says that God is powerful, violent, and partial. It identifies the Israelites as God's chosen people, who, depending on which passages are cited, are destined by God either to be *the* vehicle through which God blesses all the nations, or to dominate the nations of the world. Most common are passages that confirm the latter view, with Isaiah's words being representative:

> Your gates shall always be open;
>   day and night they shall not be shut,
> so that nations shall bring you their wealth,
>   with their kings led in procession.
> For the nation and kingdom
>   that will not serve you shall perish;
> those nations shall be utterly laid waste. (60:11–12)

Divine favoritism of one tribe over others (a central claim of Jewish, Christian, and Muslim "sacred" texts) is never a good foundation for universal blessing. Conflict is likely when groups make competing claims based on incompatible "divinely inspired" passages.

The Hebrew Scriptures identify the Jews as God's chosen. Christians also designate the Hebrew Scriptures (what Christians call the Old Testament) as part of their "sacred" text. This is true even though most Christians subordinate the teachings of the Old Testament to the New while denying the extent to which the Old, including images of a violent God, informs the New (see chapter 5). The profound influence of the Hebrew Scriptures on Christianity should be obvious. Jesus was himself a radical Jew, and Christianity originated as a reform sect within Judaism. Jewish followers of Jesus were among a minority of Jews who believed, as the Gospel writers did, that Jesus fulfilled the promises of God revealed in the Hebrew Scriptures. We will see in chapter 5 that the violence-of-God traditions in the Hebrew Bible are foundational for the Gospel writers.

The Quran in turn centrally features numerous stories and characters from both the Hebrew Bible and Christian New Testament. Muslims believe that Allah, the Arabic word for God, is the God of Abraham, Moses, Noah, the prophet Jesus, and Mary. Jews, Christians, and Muslims are all understood to be "children of Abraham," with Muslims tracing their religious descendents through Ismail (Ishmael), the firstborn son of Abraham and Hagar. The Quran is understood to be God's final word to humanity. God, according to common Muslim belief, dictated each word of the Quran to the prophet Muhammad through the angel Gabriel. God did so in order to correct the many errors of Jews and Christians, whose texts and conduct demonstrated that they had misread, distorted, misinterpreted, mistranslated, or ignored God's will.

Despite similarities and an overlay of common beliefs, one does not have to be a rocket scientist or a religious expert to see the potential for serious conflict between followers of competing monotheistic faiths. Each claims to be the locus of exclusive or decisive Truth based on competing and yet overlapping "sacred" texts. Jews claim to be God's chosen people, recipients of land, special promises, and noble mission. Christians say Jesus fulfilled Hebrew scriptural promises—a claim denied by Jews—that Jesus is the only way to God, and that evangelizing the world is a Christian obligation. Muslims believe they have received the final and definitive word from God. The Quran is Allah's divinely inspired corrective to the errors propagated through the texts and conduct of Jews and Christians. It is the religious duty of Muslims to struggle (jihad) against unbelievers in order to establish a world in accord with Allah's intent. We have one powerful God, three competing claims to Truth, three "sacred" texts revealing God's definitive will for humanity, and three groups claiming their particular understanding of universal mission is the one pleasing to God.

Jewish writer Regina Schwartz points out that monotheism has a violent legacy because it "abhors, reviles, rejects, and ejects whatever it defines as outside its compass."[6] Monotheism's hostility toward the other is rooted in the assumption that there is "a cosmic shortage of

prosperity." "Scarcity," she writes, "is encoded in the Bible as a princi-
ple of Oneness (one land, one people, one nation), and in monotheistic thinking (one Deity), it becomes a demand of exclusive allegiance
that threatens with the violence of exclusion."[7] In the context of
God's rejection or acceptance of Cain and Abel's offerings, Schwartz
asks a question about sacrifices that could with equal validity be asked
about different religions:

> What would have happened if [God] had accepted both Cain's
> and Abel's offerings instead of choosing one, and thereby pro-
> moted cooperation between the sower and the shepherd
> instead of competition and violence? What kind of God is this
> who chooses one sacrifice over the other? This God who
> excludes some and prefers others, who casts some out, is a
> monotheistic God—monotheistic not only because he demands
> allegiance to himself alone but because he confers his favor on
> one alone.[8]

UNRELENTING VIOLENCE

God's violence is relentless throughout the Hebrew Scriptures. God
orders Moses to kill disobedient children, adulterers, and a man who
"lies with a male as with a woman" (Lev 20:9–10, 13), and to stone
to death those who gather sticks on the Sabbath (Num 15:32–36).
God "blotted out every living thing that was on the face of the
ground, human beings and animals and creeping things and birds of
the air" in a genocidal flood (Gen 7:23), and made and undid a rain-
bow promise (Gen 9:16, Zeph 1:2–3). God reduces the disobedient
people to cannibalism (Lam 4:10). God sends two she-bears to maul
forty boys because they insult a prophet (2 Kings 2:23–24).

God, according to the Hebrew Scriptures, is a determined and
powerful land thief who steals from others in order to give to the
chosen people: "To your [Abram's] descendents I give this land,
from the river of Egypt to the great river, the river Euphrates, the

land of the Kenites, the Kenizzites, the Kadmonites, the Hittites, the Perizzites, the Rephaim, the Amorites, the Canaanites, the Girgashites, and the Jebusites" (Gen 15:18–21). God-ordained land thievery is accompanied by divinely sanctioned genocide. After taking the land, "You must utterly destroy them. . . . show them no mercy" (Deut 7:2). People were "massacred as an offering to Yahweh, as a form of human sacrifice" and a way of purging the land of "moral contaminants."[9]

The Hebrew Bible often portrays a male Deity plotting with male priests and male warriors. The predictable result is violence against women. God gives victory to the Israelite warrior Jephthah in exchange for the ritual sacrifice of his daughter (Judg 11). Battlefield victories and booty in goods and virgins are sanctified in the "sacred" Scriptures as part of the divine plan:

> The LORD spoke to Moses, saying, "Avenge the Israelites. . . ."
> So Moses said to the people, ". . . go against Midian, to execute
> the LORD's vengeance on Midian. . . ." They did battle against
> Midian, as the LORD had commanded Moses, and killed every
> male. . . . The Israelites took the women of Midian and their
> little ones captive; and they took all their cattle, their flocks, and
> all their goods as booty. All their towns where they had settled,
> and all their encampments, they burned, but they took all the
> spoil and all the booty, both people and animals. . . . Moses
> became angry with the officers . . . who had come from ser-
> vice in the war. Moses said to them, "Have you allowed all the
> women to live? . . . Now therefore, kill every male among the
> little ones, and kill every woman who has known a man by
> sleeping with him. But all the young girls who have not
> known a man by sleeping with him, keep alive for yourselves."
> (Num 31:1–3, 7, 9–11, 14–15, 17–18)

God wipes out Israel's enemies in service to the chosen people. God murders every firstborn in Egypt (Exod 11) and kills "the entire

army of Pharaoh" (Exod 14:28b). God also destroys the Israelites
with punishing violence when their disobedience makes them, the
chosen people, into the enemies of God:

> Then Jeremiah said to them: . . . Thus says the LORD, the God
> of Israel: I am going to turn back the weapons of war that are
> in your hands and with which you are fighting against the king
> of Babylon and against the Chaldeans who are besieging you
> outside the walls; and I will bring them together into the cen-
> ter of this city. I myself will fight against you with outstretched
> hand and mighty arm, in anger, in fury, and in great wrath. And
> I will strike down the inhabitants of this city, both human
> beings and animals; they shall die of a great pestilence. (Jer
> 21:3–6)

Pat Robertson and Jerry Falwell were rightly ridiculed for sug-
gesting that the terrorist attacks of September 11 were deserved
punishments from God. Few critics, however, were willing to challenge the numerous biblical texts that support their views. Robertson, Falwell, and others who believe the Bible demonstrates that God
withdraws protection from nations that violate God's will are right.
There is, in fact, abundant biblical evidence that says this is true. In
other words, they do not come to their conclusions by twisting texts
to justify their bizarre views. They stand on firm theological ground,
based on numerous bizarre and violent texts that are not challenged
because it is taboo to question the authority, the "sacredness," or the
"divine origin" of Scripture.

THE ENDURING ASSUMPTION

Monotheism didn't drop from the sky. It emerged over many centuries. It was the idea of late priestly writers long before it took root
in the lives of most believers in Palestine, and it was written back into
the "sacred" text, thus providing a monotheistic interpretive lens to

a polytheistic text and setting.[10] The Hebrew Bible, despite its monotheistic overlay, says that the God of Israel started out as a territorial, tribal, warrior god who competed with other gods for people's allegiance. This is clear in the logic employed by Jephthah when he refuses to discuss a land dispute with an Ammonite ruler on the grounds that Yahweh won it fair and square and gave it to the Israelites. Any complaints should be directed to their own god Chemosh:

> The LORD, the God of Israel, has conquered the Amorites for the benefit of his people Israel. Do you intend to take their place? Should you not possess what your god Chemosh gives you to possess? And should we not be the ones to possess everything that the Lord our God has conquered for our benefit? (Judg 11:23–24)

The transition from many gods in a polytheistic setting to one powerful God within a monotheistic one left a tragic and troubling legacy: Competition between gods was understood to have been won based on superior violence. It was superior violence that manifested God's holiness, established God's legitimacy, and inspired belief:

> "Who is like you, O LORD, among the gods?
>   Who is like you, majestic in holiness,
>   awesome in splendor, doing wonders?
> You stretched out your right hand,
>   the earth swallowed them. . . .
> Terror and dread fell upon them." (Exod 15:11–12, 16a)

God wiped out the armies of Egypt so that the people "would acknowledge that the LORD is God; there is no other besides him" (Deut 4:35). Isaiah 6:3 presents God as gloriously violent: "Holy, holy, holy is the LORD of Hosts [Yahweh Sabaoth, the god of armies]; the whole earth is full of his glory." God in the Exodus story creates opportunities to prove his credentials through superior violence:

Then I will harden the hearts of the Egyptians so that they will go in after them; and so I will gain glory for myself over Pharaoh and all his army, his chariots, and his chariot drivers. And the Egyptians shall know that I am the LORD, when I have gained glory for myself over Pharaoh, his chariots, and his chariot drivers. (Exod 14:17–18)

God instructs Moses to tell Pharaoh why God had let Pharaoh live:

For this time I will send all my plagues upon you yourself, and upon your officials, and upon your people, so that you may know that there is no one like me in all the earth. For by now I could have stretched out my hand and struck you and your people with pestilence, and you would have been cut off from the earth. But this is why I have let you live: to show you my power, and to make my name resound through all the earth. (Exod 9:14–16)

Superior violence inspires belief. "Israel saw the great work that the LORD did against the Egyptians. So the people feared the LORD and believed in the LORD and in his servant Moses" (Exod 14:31). So strong was the connection between God and superior violence that the overwhelming definition of salvation in the Hebrew Scriptures is the defeat of enemies:

Thus the LORD *saved* Israel that day from the Egyptians;
and Israel saw the Egyptians dead on the seashore.
     (Exod 14:30, emphasis added)

Then Moses and the Israelites sang this song to the LORD:
"I will sing to the LORD, for he has triumphed gloriously;
     horse and rider he has thrown into the sea.
The LORD is my strength and my might,
     and he has become *my salvation*. . . .

The LORD is a warrior;
the LORD is his name.
Pharaoh's chariots and his army he cast into the sea."
(Exod 15:1–4a, emphasis added)

Foreigners lost heart,
and came trembling out of their strongholds.
The LORD lives! Blessed be my rock,
and exalted be the God of *my salvation,*
the God who gave me vengeance
and subdued peoples under me;
who delivered me from my enemies.
(Ps 18:45–48a, emphasis added)

It will be said on that day,
Lo, this is our God; we have waited for him, so that he might *save us.*
This is the LORD for whom we have waited;
let us be glad and rejoice in his *salvation.*
For the hand of the LORD will rest on this mountain.
The Moabites shall be trodden down in their place
as straw is trodden down in a dung-pit.
(Isa 25:9–10, emphasis added)

Exclusive claims and tendencies inherent in monotheism are more or less destructive depending on the characteristics of the one God who is the subject of allegiance and devotion. Real problems intensify dramatically because God is understood in the Hebrew Bible, the Christian New Testament, and the Quran to be powerful, and because power is identified with violence. There are many similarities and differences to be found in the "sacred" texts of Jews, Christians, and Muslims. One point of undisputed agreement, unfortunately, is that God's overwhelming character is that of a violent, punishing, pathological Deity who uses unfathomable violence to both reward and punish, either within history or at history's end.

NOTES

1. Except as otherwise noted, citations from the Hebrew Bible and the Christian New Testament are from the NRSV (1989; see copyright page, above): Michael D. Coogan, ed., *The New Oxford Annotated Bible: New Revised Standard Version with the Apocrypha* (3d ed.; New York: Oxford University Press, 2001); online NRSV, http://www.devotions.net/bible/00bible.htm.

2. It isn't my intention to say that violence-of-God traditions are the only traditions in the Bible and the Quran. It is my intent to demonstrate that violence-of-God traditions overwhelm other aspects of these traditions. Unless the violence-of-God traditions are named, exposed, and countered, there is little hope that other aspects of these traditions—including peace, compassion, justice, community, and equity—will find meaningful expression.

3. Jack Nelson-Pallmeyer, *Jesus against Christianity: Reclaiming the Missing Jesus* (Harrisburg: Trinity Press International, 2001), 91.

4. Ibid., 76.

5. Richard Horsley, *Jesus and the Spiral of Violence: Popular Jewish Resistance in Roman Palestine* (Minneapolis: Fortress, 1993), 14, emphasis in original.

6. Regina M. Schwartz, *The Curse of Cain: The Violent Legacy of Monotheism* (Chicago: University of Chicago Press, 1997) 63.

7. Ibid., 3.

8. Ibid.

9. Stephen L. Harris, *Understanding the Bible* (5th ed.; Mountain View, Calif.: Mayfield Publishing Company, 2000), 150–51.

10. For a more detailed examination of this phenomenon, see the chapter "Messy Monotheism: False Portraits of God and Scripture," in Nelson-Pallmeyer *Jesus against Christianity*. Also see Richard Elliott Friedman, *Who Wrote the Bible?* (San Francisco: HarperSanFrancisco, 1987).

4. Violent Story Lines
in the Hebrew Scriptures

The LORD, the God of Israel, has conquered the Amorites for the benefit of his people Israel. (Judg 11:23a)

For it was the LORD's doing to harden their hearts so that they would come against Israel in battle, in order that they might be utterly destroyed, and might receive no mercy, but be exterminated, just as the LORD had commanded Moses. (Josh 11:20)

From the days of our ancestors to this day we have been deep in guilt, and for our iniquities we, our kings, and our priests have been handed over to the kings of the lands, to the sword, to captivity, to plundering, and to utter shame, as is now the case. (Ezra 9:7)

Many of those who sleep in the dust of the earth shall awake, some to everlasting life, and some to shame and everlasting contempt. (Dan 12:2)

IN CHAPTER 3 I LIFTED UP IMAGES OF GOD and violence in the Hebrew Scriptures. The characteristics of many gods in a polytheistic setting were grafted onto one, powerful Deity as monotheistic ideas took hold, first in the minds of priestly writers who controlled the "sacred" text, and later on the ground in Palestine. The principal character trait of the composite God that emerged was violence. God in the midst of many competitors proved to be God through superior violence.

Priestly writers tried to make sense out of historical highs (real and imagined) and historical lows by placing violent images of God at the heart of the three key story lines in the Hebrew Bible: the exodus, the exile, and the apocalyptic worldview. The present chapter examines the violence-of-God traditions within these story lines that carry over into the New Testament, including interpretations of Jesus' life, death, and resurrection (chapter 5), and the Quran (chapter 6).

THE EXODUS

The account of the exodus can be considered the most important story in the Bible. Whenever and wherever it was remembered, it was intended to convey a worldview similar to this: A liberating God heard the cries of an oppressed people and intervened in history to help them. Despite seemingly insurmountable obstacles, God's chosen people were destined for greatness and freedom. With divine power God defeated a cruel Egyptian Pharaoh and his army, freed the Israelites from slavery, and helped them take control of a land occupied by others, a land in which they were to be God's people. God made a covenant with them, saying that if Israel was faithful, then it would be a blessing to all the nations or would triumph over the nations.

According to many liberation readings of the book of Exodus, God is a powerful, anti-imperial Deity who takes sides with slaves, destroys superior armies, and delivers God's chosen into a land of milk and honey. God crushes or helps the chosen people to defeat enemies who stand in the way of fulfilling Israelite needs and the divine plan. According to this interpretation, the exodus is a story about God's *liberating violence*. God's violence and human violence done in God's name are the legitimate and preferred means to justice. God's liberating violence defeats empires and achieves victory for the oppressed.

For many practical, historical, and textual reasons, this traditional interpretation of the exodus needs to be challenged.[1] First, a liberation reading reinforces a violence-of-God tradition, justifies human violence done in God's name, and legitimates violent means as the way to achieve justice. Some oppressed people may take comfort in a biblical story that purports to place divine power in their camp. But we should remember that Native Americans were wiped out by European settlers who understood Indians as Canaanites, Indian land as the equivalent to Canaan, and themselves as God's chosen people. As Robert Allen Warrior writes:

> Many Puritan preachers were fond of referring to Native Americans as Amalekites and Canaanites—in other words, people who, if they would not be converted, were worthy of annihilation. By examining such instances in theological and political writings, in sermons, and elsewhere, we can understand how America's self-image as a "chosen people" has provided a rhetoric to mystify domination.[2]

A second challenge to a liberation reading of the exodus is the problem of false hope. Traditional interpretations promise divine aid in the struggle against oppression. Remembering the spiral of violence discussed briefly in chapter 2, we can say that a liberation reading encourages rebellion. The oppressed (violence 1) should rebel (violence 2) because God will fight on their behalf (violence 5). In real as opposed to fantasy history, however, violent rebellion prompts repression (violence 3). Oppressed people who violently resist injustice almost always lose because those responsible for oppressive systems generally hold overwhelming advantages in lethal power. Violent resistance justifies repression and often insures defeat. The prominent legacy of the vicious spiral of violence—oppression, rebellion, repression—is the dysfunctional violence of daily life that accompanies the breakdown of community (violence 4). There are effective nonviolent options to overcome injustice (see chapter 8), but they are ignored at least in part because the "sacred" texts of Judaism, Christianity, and Islam reflect oppressive, male understandings of power based on coercive violence.[3] Clinging to the false hope of redemptive or "liberating violence" enshrined in "sacred" stories and texts only serves to deepen the spiral of violence.

William Herzog names Jesus' parable in Mark 12:1–12 "Peasant Revolt and the Spiral of Violence." Jesus, Herzog says, told this parable to illustrate the futility of violent rebellion in the context of Rome-dominated first-century Palestine.[4] A man plants a vineyard, builds a watchtower, leases it to tenants, and leaves. At harvesttime he sends a slave to collect his share. The workers seize the slave, beat him, and send him away empty-handed. The vineyard owner sends another slave, who is beaten and insulted, and then others, whom the tenants kill. Finally, the vineyard owner sends his son to collect his share of the harvest. The workers "seized him, killed him, and threw him out of the vineyard" (v. 8). Jesus then asks and answers an ominous question: "What then will the owner of the vineyard do? He will come and destroy the tenants and give the vineyard to others" (v. 9).

People in Palestine were losing their land due to indebtedness. Rich landowners took the land and often planted vineyards in order to raise an exportable commodity: grapes turned into wine. The displaced peasants fell into destitution or were forced by necessity to work the land they formerly owned, now on behalf of wealthy, absentee owners. As Jesus told this parable, some who heard it may have experienced a sense of power and joy as the workers did what they themselves wanted to do: carry out what must have seemed just retribution against the vineyard owner's servants and his son. As Herzog points out, "The parable provided its hearers with a vicarious experience of striking back: first, the hearers vicariously beat, brutalized, and killed the hated retainers; then, they attacked the son who would inherit what was once their land."[5]

One senses the exhilaration of the oppressed tenants and those living vicariously through its telling. They who are humiliated humiliate others. They who are shamed shame others. They who are killed or considered disposable kill and dispose of the body of the owner's son. They who are the disinherited rightful heirs to the land deny the inheritance of an illegitimate heir. There must have been a feeling of power as oppression gave way to rebellion and the vicarious experience of justified revenge. If the parable had ended here, Jesus' hearers may have joined together and gone on a rampage against any deserving oppressor. But Jesus' parable includes an ominous question and response: "What then will the owner of the vineyard do? He will come and destroy the tenants and give the vineyard to others" (12:9). Oppression (violence 1) gives rise to rebellion (violence 2) and leads to repression (violence 3) and the crushing defeat of the oppressed.

False hope rooted in the liberating-violence motif of the exodus was grounded in historical fantasies. Despite its central place in the Hebrew Bible, there is no historical evidence for the exodus or the conquest. "Conquering the Canaanites," as Regina M. Schwartz writes, "was a fantasy of an exiled people,"[6] a "wild fantasy written by a powerless dispossessed people who dream of wondrous victories over their enemies, of living in a land where milk and honey flow, and of entering that land with the blessing and support of an Almighty Deity."[7] Like plutonium, however, the text has a dangerous afterlife. It not only offers false hope based on promises of God's liberating violence; it also theologically sanctions conquest. As Schwartz says, one people is created "through the massive displacement and destruction of other peoples . . . laying claim to a land that had belonged to others," and conducting a "bloody conquest under the banner of divine will."[8]

Other challenges to a liberation reading of the exodus are embedded in the texts themselves. Most interpretations sanitize the violence-of-God traditions at the heart of the exodus in favor of liberation readings. This requires turning a blind eye to many problems and contradictions in the text itself. God cannot legitimately be understood as an anti-imperial Deity who hates slavery when God blessed the biblical hero Joseph, who served Pharaoh and impoverished and enslaved all Egyptians (Gen 47); when God's murder of the firstborn Egyptians that gave rise to the Passover ritual included "the firstborn of the female slave who is behind the handmill" (Exod 11:5); or when the legal code of the Israelites said Israelites could enslave non-Israelites (Lev 25).

Tribal rivalries, human distortion, and ethnic bias lie at the heart of the book of Exodus and its depiction of God. It is okay for Joseph and other Israelites to cooperate with and benefit from Pharaoh's rule at the expense of impoverished Egyptians. It is not okay for Pharaoh to oppress Israelites. It is okay for Israelites to have slaves from foreign nations and from among resident aliens (and for God to murder Egyptian slaves as part of the killing of the firstborn), but it is not okay for Israelites to be enslaved by foreigners or to hold other Israelites as slaves. These abuses of power and ethnically based distinctions clash sharply with the exodus paradigm that Yahweh's opposition to empire, slavery, and injustice separates Yahweh from other gods. They also undermine claims that Yahweh's violence is justifiable because it is liberating violence that breaks traditional links between religion and empire, God and oppression.

These objections to a liberation reading of the exodus need to be taken seriously. We are unlikely to break the spiral of violence in real history until we challenge the sanctification of violence in our "sacred" texts. These objections, however, do not negate the fact that the exodus understood as a story of God's liberating violence was at the heart of the Hebrew Bible and the Christian New Testament. Yahweh, according to a liberation reading of the exodus, was in solidarity with oppressed Israelites, deeply concerned about their material needs, ethnically partial, and militarily powerful. The centrality of these beliefs is what made it so difficult for the priestly writers to explain why the "chosen people" lost their land and why they were crushed by one foreign empire after another.

EXILE

Exile is the second key story line in the Hebrew Scriptures that profoundly shaped violent images of God. Liberation themes of God's preferential violence may make sense to people who rout their enemies or may offer comfort to those longing to do so. The problem for the biblical writers was how to explain why history rarely if ever conformed to the lofty expectations that flowed from liberation portrayals of God as partial and powerful. Richard Horsley describes how little actual freedom there was for the people of Israel throughout much of their history:

> The Jews of Jesus' day were a subject people. Ever since the fall of Jerusalem to the Babylonian armies in 587 B.C.E., Jewish society had been subject to one imperial regime after another. The Babylonians destroyed the original Temple of Solomon, deported the ruling class to Babylon, and thus brought the Davidic dynasty to an end. When the Persians conquered Babylon in 540 B.C.E., they reversed the Babylonian imperial policy by allowing the Judean and other indigenous ruling classes to return to their native countries. Although the Persian empire thus appears relatively benign in our sources, most of which were produced by the governing elite, Judea remained a subject territory. Alexander the Great and his Macedonian armies, who conquered all territory from Greece to Egypt and India in the 330s B.C.E., did not simply bring yet another foreign political rule but imposed a cultural imperialism as well. . . . Indeed, the Jewish aristocracy's attempt to implement a Hellenizing "reform" in 175 B.C.E. touched off the massive popular Maccabean revolt (after 168) that asserted the independence of Judean society once again. Yet the tiny country ruled now semi-independently by the Maccabean or Hasmonean high priest was still part of a larger imperial system. As the Hellenistic empire of the Seleucids declined, the Romans exerted their

influence and finally conquered the whole eastern Mediterranean, including Palestine, in 63 B.C.E. Thereafter, whether through the Herodian client kings or the collaborating Jewish priestly aristocracy, the Romans controlled affairs in Jewish society.[9]

It was during their exile in Babylon (after 587 B.C.E.), a time of powerlessness, loss, and subjugation, that priestly writers turned the apparently defeated tribal, territorial deity Yahweh into the one Almighty God. If God were all-powerful and in control of history, as these priestly writers believed, then Yahweh was responsible for everything that happened. God controlled history through both *liberating and punishing violence.* Exile is a story of grief, loss, and a sense of powerlessness. In this setting, priestly writers idealized the exodus as a story of God's superior violence freeing an oppressed people, and they explained the exile as a consequence of the people's sin.

If exodus was a story of God's *liberating violence,* then the exile was a story of *God's punishing violence.* If God was all-powerful and in control of history and history turned sour, then historical catastrophes had to be Yahweh's doing. Obey Yahweh and prosper. Disobey Yahweh and suffer. This simplistic worldview and the violent images of God on which it rests have infected the "sacred" texts of Jews, Christians, and Muslims. They are evident in this representative passage from Leviticus:

> If you follow my statutes and keep my commandments and observe them faithfully, I will give you your rains in their season, and the land shall yield its produce, and the trees of the field shall yield their fruit. Your threshing shall overtake the vintage, and the vintage shall overtake the sowing; you shall eat your bread to the full, and live securely in your land. And I will grant peace in the land, and you shall lie down, and no one shall make you afraid; I will remove dangerous animals from the land, and no sword shall go through your land. You shall

give chase to your enemies, and they shall fall before you by the sword. . . .

But if you will not obey me, and do not observe all these commandments, if you spurn my statutes, and abhor my ordinances, so that you will not observe all my commandments, and you break my covenant, I in turn will do this to you: I will bring terror on you; consumption and fever that waste the eyes and cause life to pine away. You shall sow your seed in vain, for your enemies shall eat it. I will set my face against you, and you shall be struck down by your enemies; your foes shall rule over you, and you shall flee though no one pursues you. And if in spite of this you will not obey me, I will continue to punish you sevenfold for your sins. . . .

I myself will strike you sevenfold for your sins. I will bring the sword against you, executing vengeance for the covenant; and if you withdraw within your cities, I will send pestilence among you, and you shall be delivered into enemy hands. . . .

You shall eat the flesh of your sons, and you shall eat the flesh of your daughters. I will destroy your high places and cut down your incense altars; I will heap your carcasses on the carcasses of your idols. I will abhor you. I will lay your cities waste, will make your sanctuaries desolate, and I will not smell your pleasing odors. I will devastate the land, so that your enemies who come to settle in it shall be appalled at it. And you I will scatter among the nations, and I will unsheathe the sword against you; your land shall be a desolation, and your cities a waste. (Lev 26:3–7, 14–18, 24b–25, 29–33)

Promise and threat: If you obey, then all will go well; if you disobey, then you'll pay a horrible price. Time after time the biblical writers explained the exile as deserved punishment for human disobedience. Priests and prophets were powerful because they claimed to speak for God, to know where and to whom and with what kind of sacrifices and human behavior people could atone for sin, avoid

God's wrath, and trigger God's liberating violence. Their competing perspectives confused the people and blamed them for historical catastrophes. Priestly and prophetic explanations for exile were hard to reconcile with the exodus tradition's celebration of God's liberating power on behalf of a "chosen people." Jeremiah captured the depth of the contradiction posed by exile: "Who is wise enough to understand this?" he asked. "To whom has the mouth of the LORD spoken, so that they may declare it? Why is the land ruined and laid waste like a wilderness, so that no one passes through?" (9:12). God answers these questions with words that became standard explanations for exile:

> The LORD says: Because they have forsaken my law that I set before them, and have not obeyed my voice, or walked in accordance with it, but have stubbornly followed their own hearts and have gone after the Baals, as their ancestors taught them. Therefore thus says the LORD of hosts, the God of Israel: I am feeding this people with wormwood, and giving them poisonous water to drink. I will scatter them among nations that neither they nor their ancestors have known; and I will send the sword after them, until I have consumed them. (Jer 9:13–16)

Many hundreds of biblical passages reinforce violence-of-God traditions by stating and restating similar views.[10] In light of God's punishing violence, explanations for exile are often followed by *promises of a glorious reversal* in which the punishing violence of God gives way to a new round of God's "liberating violence." Empires used by God to punish the disobedient people (Isa 9; Jer 25) will themselves be laid waste by God (Isa 10). "I will make your oppressors eat their own flesh," the prophet Isaiah says, "and they shall be drunk with their own blood as with wine. Then all flesh shall know that I am the LORD your Savior and your Redeemer, the Mighty One of Jacob" (49:26).

> Foreigners shall build up your walls, and their kings shall minister to you; for in my wrath I struck you down, but in my favor

I have had mercy on you. Your gates shall always be open; day and night they shall not be shut, so that nations shall bring you their wealth, with their kings led in procession. For the nation and kingdom that will not serve you shall perish; those nations shall be utterly laid waste. (Isa 60:10–12)

The violence of God was deadly and circular. God proved to be God through superior violence, defeated Pharaoh and his armies, and planted the chosen people in a land occupied by others. When the people did something wrong, God used empires to punish them, sent them into exile as a consequence of disobedience, and then promised to destroy those empires as part of a glorious historical reversal. Fulfillment of God's promises depended always on God's violence. Liberating violence gave way to punishing violence, which gave way to a new round of liberating violence in which the oppressed people of God would become oppressors. The problem historically was that the reversal promised by priests and prophets never materialized. This gave rise to the third key story line in which expectations of God's violence reached new heights as the apocalyptic worldview joined the exodus and exile stories at the heart of the Hebrew Scriptures.

APOCALYPTICISM

The biblical writers overwhelmingly affirm the simplistic view of the world described above: obey God and be blessed, or disobey God and be punished. They also offer evidence that this worldview was unacceptable to some.[11] The biggest crack in the traditional worldview of orderly blessing and curse was a new apocalyptic theology laid out most clearly in the book of Daniel. Daniel contains both a restatement of the traditional theology and a new theology offering alternative explanations for the historical catastrophe of his people.[12]

Apocalyptic theology responded generally to many centuries of unfulfilled promises and specifically to the oppressive governance of Antiochus IV, a Seleucid ruler who around 167–164 B.C.E. ordered Jews under penalty of death to stop practicing their religion. Antiochus turned the Jewish temple into a worship center for Zeus, and he began to slaughter Jews who resisted his decrees.

There is within the book of Daniel a nonapocalyptic stream that repeats much of the old theology. The "Most High God has sovereignty over the kingdom of mortals, and sets over it whomever he will" (5:21b). This implies that oppressive rulers, including Antiochus, are instruments of God's punishments. The present catastrophe is explained by nonapocalyptic Daniel in reference to the fact that "the curse and the oath written in the law of Moses, the servant of God, have been poured out upon us, because we have sinned" (9:11). "So the LORD kept watch over this calamity until he brought it upon us. Indeed, the LORD our God is right in all that he has done; for we have disobeyed his voice" (9:14). Nonapocalyptic Daniel offers reassuring stories of a lions' den and a fiery furnace, in which sufficient faith means divine protection (6:23; 3:27). He refers to the exodus (9:15) and restates an old promise about a ruler to come who will have everlasting dominion (7:13–14).[13]

These traditional stories and explanations were discredited on the ground where the most faithful of the faithful of Jews were being slaughtered by Antiochus. Daniel responded by articulating an alternative, apocalyptic stream in which the violence-of-God tradition found new expression. Daniel's apocalyptic worldview broke new ground in three ways.

First, in the realm of cosmology, Daniel insisted that God was waging a battle with the forces of evil in heaven. This warfare mirrored and influenced earthly events. In essence, Daniel said that God didn't want the people to be oppressed by Antiochus or other imperial rulers, but God was preoccupied with heavenly struggles. God would eventually triumph against the forces of evil in heaven; until then, the people could not expect justice on earth. Evil empires would dominate history for a time, but the people could live, risk death, and die with the assurance that oppressive rulers would one day be defeated (7:23, 25–26).

A second innovation is that apocalyptic Daniel announced that a future and imminent violent coming of God would resolve the problem of human evil, not within time, but at the end of history. God's intervention would end history (8:17; 10:14; 11:35; 12:13) rather than restore Israel to historical prominence, as the prophets and priestly writers had promised. The good news was that faith in God's violence, central to the story lines of exodus and exile, would be rewarded; and that the promised victory over the forces of evil, first in heaven and then on earth, would be consummated very soon. The bad news was that historical evil was so out of control that human beings couldn't do much about it. The best they could do was to stand firm, practice their faith, and wait for the imminent violent coming of God.[14]

Apocalypticism's third innovation was that it placed resurrection front and center in the Jewish tradition for the first time. As Babylonian captivity gave way to Persian control of Palestine, Judaism assimilated the idea of resurrection from Zoroastrianism. The apocalyptic stream of Daniel offered resurrection as an alternative to the divine protection stories, in which sufficient faith resulted in safety amid lions' dens and fiery furnaces. Resurrection meant divine vindication, not protection. The promise of resurrection was a way of reestablishing God's credibility and reaffirming God's integrity. History was oppressive, but God would vindicate the lives and deaths of the faithful and punish evil people at the end of history:

> At that time Michael, the great prince, the protector of your people, shall arise. There shall be a time of anguish, such as has never occurred since nations first came into existence. But at that time your people shall be delivered, everyone who is found written in the book. Many of those who sleep in the dust of the earth shall awake, some to everlasting life, and some to shame and everlasting contempt. Those who are wise shall shine like the brightness of the sky, and those who lead many to righteousness, like the stars forever and ever. (12:1–3)

The violence-of-God traditions at the heart of the exodus, exile, and apocalyptic story lines in the Hebrew Scriptures carry over into the New Testament and the Quran. These stories make blunt distinctions between good and evil, insiders and outsiders, those deserving of rewards and punishments. The spiral of violence imbedded in these "sacred" texts spills over into human violence in real history and within Scripture itself. On behalf of the Pharaoh, Joseph uses food as a weapon. As a result, all Egyptians end up penniless, landless, and enslaved (Gen 47). Resentments flower. The powerful Israelites suffer when a new Pharaoh takes control. Hatreds explode, and as always violence thrives and survives numerous reversals. The Israelites, according to the biblical script, groan amid their oppression and with God's help fight back and win. In the aftermath of Pharaoh's defeat, lands are stolen, and "divinely sanctioned" genocide is carried out (Exod). Elijah wins a contest with the priests of Baal and then executes them (2 Kings 18:35–40). Israelites, unable to sing the Lord's song in captivity, anticipate the happy day when they will smash the heads of their captor's children against the rocks (Ps 137:9). Isaiah announces that God will one day come "with vengeance," "save" the people, and "spare no one" (35:4; 47:3). With God's help, Isaiah promises, the oppressed will become oppressors. Kings who took Jewish leaders into exile will themselves be humiliated, and the wealth of the nations will flow to Israel. "With their faces to the ground they shall bow down to you, and lick the dust of your feet" (49:23). Daniel walks away from the lions' den, and immediately "those who had accused Daniel were brought and thrown into the den of lions—they, their children, and their wives. Before they reached the bottom of the den, the lions overpowered them and broke their bones in pieces" (Dan 6:24).

In this context of a never-ending spiral of violence at the heart of violence-of-God traditions, God becomes an instrument of human revenge. Compassion and salvation are militarized, that is, understood as the crushing defeat of enemies within or at the end of history. In the apocalyptic view, God is the ultimate avenger of wrongs at the end of history rather than within it because the imperial situation makes it difficult for humans to carry out the desired punishments. The violence-of-God traditions at the center of the exodus, exile, and apocalyptic story lines in the Hebrew Bible are, contrary to the views of many Christians, at the heart of the New Testament as well.

NOTES

1. For a more complete discussion of these issues, see Jack Nelson-Pallmeyer, *Jesus against Christianity: Reclaiming the Missing Jesus* (Harrisburg: Trinity Press International, 2001), 38–53.

2. Robert Allen Warrior, "A Native American Perspective: Canaanites, Cowboys, and Indians," in R. S. Sugirtharajah, ed., *Voices from the Margin: Interpreting the Bible in the Third World* (Maryknoll, N.Y.: Orbis Books, 1991), 293.

3. The problem of men and violence may have both genetic and cultural roots. Some psychologists and sociologists argue that men genetically may be slightly more prone to violence than women, but that the most problematic variable is the culture of violence that reinforces men's predisposition to violent behavior. For an interesting discussion of these issues, see Myriam Miedzian, *Boys Will Be Boys: Breaking the Link between Masculinity and Violence* (New York: Anchor Books, 1991).

4. For an insightful interpretation of this and other parables, see William R. Herzog II, *Parables as Subversive Speech: Jesus as Pedagogue of the Oppressed* (Louisville, Ky.: Westminster/John Knox Press, 1994).

5. Ibid., 109.

6. Regina M. Schwartz, *The Curse of Cain: The Violent Legacy of Monotheism* (Chicago: University of Chicago Press, 1997), x.

7. Ibid., 57

8. Ibid.

9. Richard Horsley, *Jesus and the Spiral of Violence: Popular Jewish Resistance in Roman Palestine* (Minneapolis: Fortress, 1993), 3.

10. For a much more detailed look at biblical texts that explain the exile as God's punishment for disobedience, see *Jesus against Christianity.*

11. See, for example, the book of Job and Psalm 44.

12. For a detailed discussion of Daniel, see *Jesus against Christianity,* chapter 10.

13. See 1 Kings 11:36; 2 Kings 8:19.

14. There is scholarly dispute as to whether apocalyptic writers believed the imminent violent coming of God would mean the end of the world or the end of earthly injustice. In either case, it would mark the end of history as we know it because God would impose justice. In either case, it can also be said, the apocalyptic view turned out to be a fantasy.

5. Violence-of-God Traditions in the New Testament

And Mary said, "My soul magnifies the Lord, and my spirit rejoices in God my Savior. . . . He has shown strength with his arm; he has scattered the proud in the thoughts of their hearts. He has brought down the powerful from their thrones, and lifted up the lowly; he has filled the hungry with good things, and sent the rich away empty." (Luke 1:46–47, 51–53)

But when he saw many Pharisees and Sadducees coming for baptism, he said to them, "You brood of vipers! Who warned you to flee the wrath to come? Bear fruit worthy of repentance. . . . Even now the ax is lying at the root of the trees; every tree therefore that does not bear good fruit is cut down and thrown into the fire. . . . His winnowing fork is in his hand, and he will clear his threshing floor and will gather his wheat into the granary; but the chaff he will burn with unquenchable fire." (Matt 3:7–8, 10, 12)

We give you thanks, Lord God Almighty, who are and who were, for you have taken your great power and begun to reign.

The nations raged, but your wrath has come, and the time for judging the dead, for rewarding your servants, the prophets and saints and all who fear your name, both small and great, and for destroying those who destroy the earth. (Rev 11:17–18)

—⌐∪⌐—

ASSESSING THE VIOLENCE-OF-GOD TRADITIONS in the New Testament is complicated by two factors. First, many biblical scholars and many Christians deny the extent to which violent images of God dominate the Hebrew Scriptures and Christian New Testament. Most Christians haven't read the Bible cover to cover. Many say that Jesus fulfills promises made in the Hebrew Bible, but they minimize the degree to which those promises and Christian rituals associated with them presume God's violence. Few take the time to try to understand how, when, why, or where a Jewish Jesus affirms, revolutionizes, or breaks with his tradition, including his challenge to the violent images of God that dominate the exodus, exile, and apocalyptic story lines discussed previously. To the degree that violence is an issue, many Christians conclude that the God of the Old Testament is violent, wrathful, and judging, and that the God of the New Testament is loving, forgiving, and graceful.

The passages just cited and many more undermine this view. Mary, consistent with the promises of Isaiah, announces a long-awaited reversal in historical affairs as the result of God's liberating power. John the Baptist, like the apocalyptic writer of Daniel, divides the world into distinctive camps of good and evil and announces the imminent violent coming of God to judge, punish, and reward. The author of the book of Revelation rejoices that "Almighty God" has initiated the end time as promised in the book of Daniel and has "begun to reign," so that those who fear God can be rewarded and those who don't can be destroyed.

A second obstacle to assessing the violence-of-God traditions is a clash in perspectives that divides the historical Jesus from the New Testament writers.[1] The Gospel writers interpret the meaning of

Jesus' life, death, and resurrection through the lens of their own deeply held apocalyptic views, while leaving evidence imbedded in their accounts that the historical Jesus was nonviolent and rejected violent images of God. They paint Jesus, for example, as both apocalyptic and not apocalyptic. Both portraits can't be true.[2] In *Jesus against Christianity: Reclaiming the Missing Jesus,* I make the case that the New Testament writers betray Jesus because they interpret the meaning of his life, death, and resurrection in light of violent images of God and expectations of history that Jesus himself rejected.

The present chapter argues that the violence-of-God traditions embedded in the exodus, exile, and apocalyptic story lines of the Hebrew Scriptures are central to the New Testament as well. At the heart of these traditions is the desire to explain historical problems or to appropriate God's power in service to one's objectives. God the holy warrior will fight with us or send us a Messiah to liberate us and defeat our enemies. If we are in bondage, in exile, wiped out, or dominated by foreign empires, then God the punishing Judge is rightly punishing us for our sins; or in the apocalyptic worldview, God the violent, apocalyptic Judge is battling cosmic evil and is therefore preoccupied but will come soon to wipe out our enemies and reward us at history's end.

The violence-of-God traditions interact and overlap with each other so thoroughly throughout both the Old and New Testaments that it is difficult to isolate one from another. *God's liberating, punishing, or apocalyptic violence is the named or unnamed assumption behind nearly every passage, story, and theological claim in the New Testament.*

PUNISHING VIOLENCE

Violence-of-God traditions embedded in the key story lines of the Hebrew Scriptures presume that God is powerful, punishing, and in control of history. God the liberator punishes (defeats) enemies; God the ruthless Judge punishes the disobedient people of God; God the apocalyptic avenger of wrongs punishes evildoers at the end of history and rewards the faithful. The presumption of God's punishing violence also lies at the heart of the Christian New Testament that claims Jesus as Savior and understands the death of Jesus to be an atoning sacrifice. From what, we should ask, does Jesus save us? The classic answer is that Jesus saves us from the consequence of our sin. God loved the world so much that God sent Jesus to die for us. Believe this and be not condemned (John 3:16–17).

Many Christians see in these words a gracious God who loves us enough to send his only son to die in our place so that we might avoid our deserved punishment, go to heaven instead of hell, and have eternal life. Brutal images of God remain hidden behind these rose-colored interpretations. If we believe that Jesus died for us so that we will not be condemned, then we should ask, "Condemned by whom?" The answer is, God. What remains unstated in classic Christian statements of faith is that Jesus dies in order to save us from God, not from sin. More precisely, Jesus' sacrificial death saves us from a violent God who punishes sin.

The idea that God sent Jesus to die for our sins makes sense only if we embrace violent and punishing images of God featured prominently in the Hebrew Scriptures. The violent God of the Hebrew Scriptures and Christian New Testament requires appeasement, sacrifices, and holiness. Regina M. Schwartz argues that the "sacrifices of Cain and Abel suggest . . . an offering to ward off divine wrath, to encourage the deity's favor, to invoke his blessings of prosperity."[3] The image of Yahweh is not loving or compassionate but violent and unpredictable. Offerings and sacrifices are human attempts to appease a wrathful deity, but success is by no means assured. Abel succeeds. Cain fails. The text doesn't say why. It gives the impression that God is violent, petty, arbitrary, and to be feared.

Priestly writers say God orders disobedient children to be murdered (Lev 20:9, Deut 20:18–21) and a man who gathers sticks on the Sabbath to be stoned to death (Num 16:32–36) because they believe these actions are necessary to appease a violent deity. The overwhelming preoccupation with holiness in the priestly writings is rooted in fear that God will "vomit" unholy people out of the land

(Lev 18:24–25). Ezra, the priestly writer who may have been the redactor who gave final shape to the Torah, took the premise that God requires strict holiness—including separation from all that defiles—to its logical and troubling conclusion. After the Persian Empire allowed the Jewish ruling class to go home, Ezra explained that exile was a consequence of mixed marriages:

> [The officials said,] "The people of Israel, the priests, and the Levites have not separated themselves from the peoples of the lands. . . . For they have taken some of their daughters as wives for themselves and for their sons. Thus the holy seed has mixed itself with the peoples of the lands, and in this faithlessness the officials and leaders have led the way." . . .
>
> [I said,] "From the days of our ancestors to this day we have been deep in guilt, and for our iniquities we, our kings, and our priests have been handed over to the kings of the lands, to the sword, to captivity, to plundering, and to utter shame, as is now the case." (Ezra 9:1b, 2, 7)

The scapegoat ritual of the Day of Atonement, known as Yom Kippur, became a prominent frame of reference for sacrificial interpretations of Jesus' death. It is described in Leviticus 16 and became one of the most important of all Jewish festivals. The ritual involved two goats. One goat was slaughtered as a "sin offering" "for the LORD" (16:9, 15). The other goat was sent away "for Azazel" (a desert demon) and called "a scapegoat" because it was allowed to escape into the wilderness after having the sins of the people transferred onto it (16:8, 10 KJV). The scapegoat carried the sins of the people out of the holy land:

> When he [the high priest] has finished atoning for the holy place and the tent of meeting and the altar [by sprinkling on it blood from the sacrificed goat], he shall present the live goat. Then Aaron shall lay both his hands on the head of the live goat, and confess over it all the iniquities of the people of

Israel, and all their transgressions, all their sins, putting them on
the head of the goat, and sending it away into the wilderness
by means of someone designated for the task. The goat shall
bear on itself all their iniquities to a barren region; and the goat
shall be set free in the wilderness. (16:20–22)

The Day of Atonement was a priestly response to exile understood as God's just punishment for sin, including insufficient holiness.
This "annual observance [of Yom Kippur], so important in post-exilic
Israel, is never mentioned in the pre-exilic literature."[4] In other
words, Yom Kippur was a desperate attempt to appease a punishing
God in the context of exile. The consistency of violence-of-God traditions throughout the Bible is clear when we remember that the
New Testament writers present Jesus as the ultimate sacrificial lamb
or as the scapegoat on whom the sins of the world are placed. Jesus
stands between a wrathful deity and sinful humanity. His death sub-
stitutes for our own.

The Christian Eucharist also presumes the punishing violence of
God. The language "body" and "blood" of Christ places the Lord's
Supper in a sacrificial context, reinforcing the continuity in violence-
of-God traditions between Old and New Testaments. The Jews were
saved from divine slaughter in Egypt by marking their doorposts
with the blood of a perfect sacrificial lamb so that a violent deity
could identify and pass over their houses. Christians too will be
spared God's wrath by the perfect blood sacrifice of Jesus. Understood in a sacrificial light, the Eucharist, or Lord's Supper, ritualizes
appeasement of a bloodthirsty, punishing deity. It commemorates
Jesus' blood sacrifice in which Jesus stands between sinful humanity
and God's violent judgment.[5]

Augustine employed a similar logic in arguing that the virgin
birth had to be understood literally. Jesus, in order to appease a punishing deity, had to be born of a virgin in order to break the cycle by
which women through childbirth passed on sin from generation to
generation. Without the virgin birth, the sacrifice would not have

been perfect because Jesus would not have been born without sin. The rift between God and humanity, therefore, would not have been mended. When it was finally discovered that women had eggs and were more than divine incubators, the Catholic Church insisted, for the same reasons as noted above, that Mary had herself been immaculately conceived.[6]

Violent, punishing images and expectations of God infect the New Testament in other ways as well. God, who in the Exodus story is a capable land thief, in the book of Acts is a petty murderer. God kills Ananias and Sapphira because they withhold part of the proceeds from a voluntary land sale. Their generosity isn't rewarded. God wants all the money. By keeping some of it for themselves, they are guilty of putting "the Spirit of the Lord to the test" (Acts 5:9). You shouldn't put the Spirit of the Lord to the test any more than young boys should call a prophet "baldhead." After Ananias is told that he lied to God when he withheld part of the proceeds from the land sale, "he fell down and died. And great fear seized all who heard of it" (5:5).

The Gospel writer known as Matthew frequently places threatening and hateful words on the lips of Jesus. Like the prophet Muhammad who saddled Muslims with an unrelenting violence-of-God tradition (see chapter 6), Matthew can't seem to imagine people doing the right thing without warnings of violent judgments hanging over their heads, including threats of hell. Feed the hungry, clothe the naked, comfort the sick, and visit the imprisoned, and receive a heavenly reward. Fail to do so and you "go away into eternal punishment" (25:45–46). Matthew's Jesus consistently uses heavily apocalyptic imagery when warning the people of the imminent judgment to come:

> Just as the weeds are collected and burned up with fire, so will it be at the end of the age. The Son of Man will send his angels, and they will collect out of his kingdom all causes of sin and all evildoers, and they will throw them into the furnace of fire, where there will be weeping and gnashing of teeth. (13:40–42)

Matthew is often an unreliable witness to Jesus. In his parables Jesus repeatedly exposes key actors in the oppressive system, only to have Matthew present those exposed as "God figures" that Matthew blesses with the authority of Jesus' voice. These "God figures" consistently send people to the torturers or to other terrible punishments. Jesus' favorite activity, according to Matthew, is to threaten people with violent punishments, using his preferred phrase, "weeping and gnashing of teeth." "Then the king said to the attendants, 'Bind him hand and foot, and throw him into the outer darkness, where there will be weeping and gnashing of teeth' " (22:13). Then "the master of that slave will come on a day when he does not expect him and at an hour that he does not know. He will cut him in pieces and put him with the hypocrites, where there will be weeping and gnashing of teeth" (24:50–51). "But his master replied, 'You wicked and lazy slave! . . . As for this worthless slave, throw him into the outer darkness, where there will be weeping and gnashing of teeth' " (25:26a, 30).

THE APOCALYPTIC AND MESSIANIC SEESAW

The strength of Roman imperialism (Rome dominated Palestine from 63 B.C.E. until well after the books of the New Testament were written), Jesus' violent death (likely 30 C.E.), and the Roman destruction of Jerusalem and the Jewish temple (70 C.E.) led New Testament writers to reinforce and reshape the violence-of-God traditions at the heart of the Hebrew Scriptures. The Gospel writers, as we saw above, reaffirmed the tradition of God's punishing violence when they interpreted Jesus' death in light of atonement, blood sacrifice, and sin-bearing, scapegoat rituals. Equally prominent, however, were New Testament affirmations that Jesus life and death could best be understood in continuity with the violence-of-God traditions rooted in apocalyptic and messianic expectations.

Apocalyptic and messianic expectations ebbed and flowed throughout the historical period framed by Daniel's articulation of the apocalyptic worldview in response to Antiochus (approximately 165 B.C.E.) and writings of the New Testament (50–100 C.E.).[7] Antiochus was overthrown by Jewish freedom fighters (the Maccabees) after a protracted guerrilla war. In stark contrast to new exodus expectations and prophetic promises, however, victory did not lead to liberation, peace, and prosperity. The post-Antiochus reality on the ground in Palestine was far removed from the old Davidic promise of everlasting kingship, restated by Daniel as a promise of "everlasting dominion" (7:14), and it was equally distant from Isaiah's imperial pretensions of a historical reversal in which Israel would "possess the nations as male and female slaves" (14:2b). The Seleucid empire was defeated, but evil persisted. Following the Jewish triumph, repression, inequality, and brutal factionalism between Jewish priestly groups deepened. Evil was alive and well, but with the independent rule, it wore a transparently Jewish face.

Jewish groups interpreted the defeat of Antiochus in two distinctive ways, with each interpretation reinforcing a different violence-of-God tradition. Antiochus's defeat for some rekindled the belief in liberating violence, holy war, and salvation understood as defeat of enemies. According to Marcus Borg, the victories of the Maccabees provided "empirical verification for the claim . . . that Yahweh gives victory to the chosen people, [and] demonstrated that resistance was reasonable, even when it seemed foolish on more pragmatic grounds."[8]

Others understood things differently. Ongoing injustices and deepening hostility between different Jewish priestly factions drove the Essenes into the desert. This priestly, apocalyptic, monastic community saw the line of priest-kings associated with the Maccabees as illegitimate. The defeat of Antiochus and rise of the Maccabees didn't verify holy war. Maccabean-led injustices, according to the Essenes, were an affront to God that confirmed the historical pessimism inherent in the apocalyptic worldview. They couldn't imagine resolving differences with others within society or within history, and so the Essenes withdrew and prepared for a new violent coming of

God, at which time the present leaders of the temple would be destroyed. When Rome took control of Palestine in 63 B.C.E., the Essenes expanded the targets of God's violence to include their Roman oppressors.[9]

The Essenes "saw themselves as the only Jews who were truly faithful to Yahweh's commands," and they observed "strict regulations of purity and obedience."[10] They taught hatred of enemies and prepared for a "climactic battle between the Sons of Light and the Sons of Darkness."[11] *Their Rule of the Community* (1QSa) stated that the "man of understanding" is expected to "hate all that He (God) has despised." Members of the community were to "love all the sons of light, / each according to his lot in the Council of God; / and . . . hate all the sons of darkness, / each according to his fault in the Vengeance of God." "These are the norms of conduct for the man of understanding in these times, concerning what he must love and how he must hate. Everlasting hatred for all men of the pit because of their spirit of hoarding."[12] According to Uta Ranke-Heinemann:

> This hatred will break out in the approaching eschatological war. The end of the world, which the Qumran sect expected to come soon, would be preceded by a war of revenge and retribution, the war of the "sons of light" (the Qumran community) against the "sons of darkness." This war is described in detail in the *War Scroll* (1QM). . . . It will go on for forty years. In the first twenty years, all the foreign nations will be conquered; in the following twenty, all other Jews.[13]

Perhaps because the apocalyptic end was slow in coming, a resurgent expectation of a Davidic Messiah flowered near the time of Jesus' birth. Richard Horsley and Neil Asher Silberman describe how in "the decades immediately preceding the birth of Jesus, a wide variety of messianic visions grew more fervent and vivid among the People of Israel." These visions, like their apocalyptic counterparts, were shaped by historical failures. Because "the members of the royal house of Judah and the later Hasmonean [Maccabean] kings had proved themselves utterly powerless to live up to the responsibilities of their office and defend the people of Israel against the relentless advance of foreign empires [the latest being the Roman Empire], a radically new vision of the character of Israel's true messiah arose."[14] At this juncture historical problems temporarily led away from apocalypticism as visions of an idealized earthly ruler were revived and refined. The new vision, according to Horsley and Silberman, centered on "the arrival of a messianic figure, a new son of David, who would finally lead Israel to regain its former glory and establish the Kingdom of God."[15]

Many Jews believed that the long-awaited messianic moment had arrived following the death of Herod the Great, a Rome-appointed client king who had ruled Palestine from 37 B.C.E. until 4 B.C.E. There were rebellions throughout Palestine, and initial successes allowed the people to appoint popular kings or messiahs. The success of these "sons of David" seemed to verify the views of those who had refined the visions of an idealized Davidic ruler and seemed to confirm Isaiah's promise that God would help Israel to triumph over the nations.

Messianic fantasies came crashing down as Roman soldiers slaughtered Jews, burned cities, and lined roads with crosses on which decaying corpses became food for birds and wild animals and served to discourage future rebellions. The destruction of popular kings and messianic claimants who fought against Rome and its client regimes following Herod's death would have had devastating consequences beyond the carnage of war. It marked another failure of historical promise and of theological vision. Bad news once again, however, proved to be fertile ground for apocalypticism. Rome's triumph set the stage for John the Baptist's historically pessimistic apocalyptic movement. John warned the people of "the wrath of God" soon coming. God, with "winnowing fork . . . in his hand," was ready to "clear his threshing floor," "gather his wheat into the granary," and burn the chaff with "unquenchable fire" (Matt 3:12).

John's apocalyptic promise went unfulfilled, and he was executed by one of Herod's sons. Instead of undermining apocalyptic fantasies,

John's death, Jesus' execution, and Jerusalem's destruction, like other historical crises, deepened expectations of God's violence and led to a recasting of the apocalyptic worldview itself. Seeds of apocalyptic thought were watered by bitter tears from many crushing defeats: the failure of Daniel's vision to be realized (neither the end time nor the end of injustice materialized), injustices linked to the Maccabees, the rise of Roman power, the oppressive client-king rule of Herod, the crushing defeat of "messiahs" at the hands of Roman soldiers, and John's death. Jesus, another declared Messiah, was crucified, and Roman soldiers later burned Jerusalem and destroyed the temple.

In this context, New Testament interpretations of Jesus were rooted firmly in apocalyptic expectations that reaffirmed God's violent power. The Gospel writers were caught up in a groundswell of apocalyptic expectation for three key reasons. First, their hero Jesus had been crucified, and apocalypticism offered them a way to make sense of his death. One common explanation for Jesus' violent death was to present him as the apocalypse personified. Daniel had spoken of one like a human who would rule on God's behalf (7:13–14). The Gospel writers presented Jesus as a specific apocalyptic figure, the Son of Man, who would return soon as cosmic judge. Apocalyptic Daniel had reconciled God with brutal but temporary historical setbacks. The crucifixion was presented as an unexpected or even anticipated instrument in God's divine plan. Jesus' resurrection was the first fruit of the general resurrection anticipated by Daniel. Paul and the Gospel writers claimed that Jesus' resurrection was the beginning of the end time. Jesus was the apocalyptic "Son of Man," the cosmic judge who would return soon and oversee a final judgment. Ironically, Jesus the atoning sacrificial Lamb of God, who stood between a wrathful deity and sinful people, would return to wipe out most of humanity. Jesus, the Lamb, or returning Christ, became God's murderous apocalyptic accomplice, who would violently judge and crush enemies and evildoers at the end of history:

Then another angel, a third, followed them, crying with a loud voice, "Those who worship the beast and its image, and receive a mark on their foreheads or on their hands, they will also drink the wine of God's wrath, poured unmixed into the cup of his anger, and they will be tormented with fire and sulfur in the presence of the holy angels and in the presence of the Lamb." (Rev 14:9–10)

A second reason why the Gospel writers embraced apocalypticism is that between three and four decades *after* Jesus' murder and shortly *before* the Gospels were written, the Jewish temple and Jerusalem were destroyed in the Roman-Jewish war of 66–70 C.E. Apocalypticism offered a framework in which the destruction of temple and city could be understood as divine punishment for Jews rejecting Jesus.

A third reason the New Testament writers offered an apocalyptic interpretation of Jesus is that by the time the Gospels were written many Jews had rejected Jewish Christian claims that Jesus fulfilled God's promises as laid out in the Hebrew Scriptures. Apocalypticism served as ideological window dressing for growing Christian hatred and desired revenge. Those who repudiated Jewish Christian interpretation of Jesus did not fare well in Gospel accounts. They were blamed for the murder of Jesus, and their rejection of Jesus was used to explain Rome's destruction of Jerusalem and the temple. It was only a small step to make God's punishment permanent. Those who rejected Jesus would face the same harsh fate as all enemies of God: they would spend eternity in hell.

The above analysis should make it abundantly clear that violence-of-God traditions lie at the heart of both the Hebrew Scriptures and Christian New Testament. Unfortunately, God's violent pathology is similarly reinforced throughout the Quran.

NOTES

1. Some examples of historical Jesus scholarship include Marcus Borg, *Jesus: A New Vision* (San Francisco: Harper & Row, 1987); John Dominic Crossan, *Jesus: A Revolutionary Biography* (San Francisco: HarperSanFrancisco, 1995); Robert W. Funk et al., *The Five Gospels: What Did Jesus Really Say?* (Santa Rosa, Calif.: Polebridge, 1993); and Jack Nelson-Pallmeyer, *Jesus against Christianity* (Harrisburg: Trinity Press International, 2001).

2. For a discussion of whether or not Jesus was apocalyptic, see Robert J. Miller, ed., *The Apocalyptic Jesus: A Debate* (Santa Rosa, Calif.: Polebridge, 2001).

3. Regina M. Schwartz, *The Curse of Cain: The Violent Legacy of Monotheism* (Chicago: University of Chicago Press, 1997), 2.

4. Raymond E. Brown, ed., et al., *The Jerome Biblical Commentary* (Englewood Cliffs, N.J.: Prentice-Hall, 1968), 77.

5. For a description and critique of various atonement theories that have emerged throughout church history, see Delores Williams, *Sisters in the Wilderness* (Maryknoll, N.Y.: Orbis Books, 1993), 161–70.

6. John Shelby Spong, *Why Christianity Must Change or Die* (San Francisco: HarperSanFrancisco, 1998), 94.

7. Paul's genuine letters were probably written between 50 and 62 C.E.; most other New Testament books, including three Gospels, the book of Acts, and Revelation, were written in the three decades following the Roman destruction of the Jewish temple. The Gospel of Mark may have been written between 66 and 70 C.E. and 2 Peter around 150 C.E. See Stephen L. Harris, *Understanding the Bible* (5th ed.; Mountain View, Calif.: Mayfield Publishing Company, 2000), 353–54.

8. Marcus Borg, *Conflict, Holiness, and Politics in the Teachings of Jesus* (New York: Edwin Mellen, 1984), 55.

9. The compound of the Essenes was destroyed in 68 C.E. by the Romans, but not before the community hid its library. In 1947 and later years, the library was found hidden in caves near Qumran, just northeast of the Dead Sea.

10. Harris, *Understanding the Bible*, 20, 40.

11. Ibid., 40.

12. Uta Ranke-Heinemann, *Putting Away Childish Things* (San Francisco: HarperSanFranscisco, 1995), 259.

13. Ibid.

14. Richard A. Horsley et al., *The Message and the Kingdom: How Jesus and Paul Ignited a Revolution and Transformed the Ancient World* (New York: Grossett/Putnam, 1997), 15.

15. Ibid., 14–15.

6. Violence-of-God Traditions in the Quran

Woe to each sinful Dealer in Falsehoods: He hears the Signs Of Allah rehearsed to him, Yet is obstinate and lofty, As if he had not Heard them: then announce To him a Penalty Grievous! And when he learns Something of Our Signs, He takes them in jest: For such there be A humiliating Penalty. In front of them is Hell: and of no profit To them is anything They may have earned, Nor any protectors they May have taken to themselves Besides Allah: for them Is a tremendous Penalty. This is (true) Guidance: And for those who reject The Signs of their Lord, Is a grievous Penalty Of abomination. (Quran 45:7–11)[1]

Then fight in Allah's cause—Thou are held responsible Only for thyself—And rouse the Believers. It may be that Allah Will restrain the fury Of the Unbelievers; For Allah is the strongest In might and in punishment. (4:84)

And Allah turned back The Unbelievers for (all) Their fury: no advantage Did they gain: and enough Is Allah for the Believers In their fight. And Allah is full of Strength, Able to

73

enforce His Will. And those of the people Of the Book who aided Them—Allah did take them Down from their strongholds And cast terror into Their hearts, (so that) Some ye slew, and some Ye made prisoners. And he made you heirs Of their lands, their houses, And their goods, And a land which Ye had not frequented (Before). And Allah has Powers over all things. (33:25–27)

—ⁿ∫—

THESE AND MANY OTHER VERSES IN THE QURAN indicate that violence-of-God traditions are not limited to the "sacred texts" of Jews and Christians. Allah sends unbelievers to a fiery hell. Strongest in might, Allah restrains the power of unbelievers and delivers their land, houses, and other booty to the faithful. Images of an all-powerful, violent God *dominate* the Quran as they do the Bible. Allah is "Master of the Day of Judgment" (1:3), has "perfect knowledge" (2:29), has "power over all things" (2:109), has "dominion of the heavens And the earth" (2:107), is "well-acquainted With the wrongdoers" (2:95), and delivers "a grievous punishment" to "those without faith" (2:104).

The Quran begins each *surah* (chapter, sura) with comforting words: "In the name of Allah, the Beneficent, the Merciful." It is surprising, therefore, that the actual text of nearly every sura uses images of a wrathful, punishing God to condition human behavior. Under the sanction of divine wrath, Muslims are urged to do many things, including believe in Allah and his prophet (2:4–7), help orphans (4:8–10), and slaughter enemies (8:67). God's violence or threatened violence often spills over into human violence done in service to God's will.

PERVASIVE VIOLENCE

I sometimes ask students randomly to select and read a psalm in order to make a point about expectations of God's violence. On the first or second try, they generally encounter verses in which salvation is understood specifically as defeat of enemies. In a similar way, almost every sura in the Quran presents fear of God's wrath as the foundation for belief and action. Muhammad, like Matthew, seems unable to imagine people behaving ethically or living out what he understands to be God's will without the threat of divine sanction. Matthew's Jesus encourages compliance with his demands by threatening people with gruesome punishments, including "weeping and gnashing of teeth." Muhammad's Allah advocates specific actions and threatens people guilty of noncompliance with an "awful doom "or "grievous penalty."

God's violence or threatened violence is so pervasive in the Quran that it is difficult to capture its full weight or describe its many manifestations. In the remainder of this chapter, I describe the violence-of-God traditions in the Quran in relation to seven related categories: Threats of punishment in hell linked to disbelief; threats of punishment in hell linked to poor conduct or used to motivate positive behavior; fear of God rooted in stories similar to biblical accounts of God's punishing violence; justified human violence and warfare against religious others and enemies; violence rooted in promises of paradise for believers, including those killed in battle; images of God as holy warrior; and a brief look at additional passages that could have reasonably been cited by those who carried out the terrorist attacks on September 11, 2001.

THREATS OF HELL LINKED TO DISBELIEF

The heart of Muslim belief is that there is no God but God and Muhammad is God's prophet. All guidelines for living contained in the Quran are based on the reliability of this proclamation. Belief or disbelief determines one's ultimate fate. If Allah is the only God, if Allah is as powerful as the Quran says, if Muhammad is Allah's final and most important prophet, and if the Quran is God's final revelation to humanity—then you must listen to and abide by what the book and the prophet say. "This is the Book; In it is guidance sure,

without doubt, To those who fear Allah" (2:2). "But those who reject
Faith And belie Our Signs, They shall be Companions of the Fire;
They shall abide therein" (2:39). As for disbelievers, "Great is the
penalty they (incur)" (2:7). "And who believe in the Revelation Sent
to thee, And sent before thy time, And (in their hearts) Have the
assurance of the Hereafter. They are on (true guidance), From their
Lord, and it is These who will prosper" (2:4–5). "Then fear the Fire
Whose fuel is Men and Stones—Which is prepared for those Who
reject Faith. But give glad tidings To those who believe And work
righteousness, That their portion is Gardens, Beneath which rivers
flow" (2:24b–25a). "For Allah will Collect the Hypocrites and those
Who defy Faith—all in Hell" (4:140).

Similar threats directed to disbelievers and rewards promised to
believers are featured in hundreds of passages. The violent images of
God standing behind them are troubling for many reasons, such as
these two: First, spiritual violence (violence 5; see chapter 2, above) is
central to the Quran. Spiritual violence has many dimensions. In the
present context, it is embodied in Muhammad and Allah's unrelenting threats of hell and fire, used to condition human behavior.

Second, the verses cited above and similar verses throughout the
Quran reinforce many aspects of the violence-of-God traditions discussed in relation to the Hebrew Scriptures and Christian New Testament. Allah is the sovereign of history and can do all things. Allah
the holy warrior gives the faithful blessings, booty, and heavenly
rewards. Allah chastises the unfaithful with failure now and eternal
punishment later. "Not a leaf doth fall But with His knowledge"
(6:59). "Say: 'O my people! Do whatever ye can: I will do (my part):
Soon will ye know Who it is whose end Will be (best) in the Hereafter: Certain it is that The wrongdoers will not prosper' " (6:135).

If you are faithful, then you can expect to succeed in this world
and/or be rewarded in paradise. If you are unfaithful, then you will
likely experience hardship now and/or be sent to the fire in the
hereafter. These sentiments and the images of God that lie behind
them parallel priestly explanations for exile (see Lev 26) and apocalyptic promises that God's violence will destroy wrongdoers and

vindicate the faithful at the end time. This tidy and simplistic view of life is based on God's absolute power and on rigid distinctions between good and evil, belief and disbelief. It can fuel conflict, encourage intolerance, and justify violence whenever historical reality doesn't conform to expectations that flow from the theology and worldview of the Quran.

Like the prophets and priestly writers of the Bible, the Quran promises a well-ordered universe. Allah "will defend thee From men (who mean mischief). For Allah guideth not Those who reject Faith" (5:67). "If Allah touch thee with affliction, none Can remove it but He; If He touch thee with happiness, He hath power over all things" (6:17). "It is those who believe And confuse not their beliefs With wrong—that are (Truly) in security, for they Are on (right) guidance" (6:82). "He May reward with justice Those who believe And work righteousness; But those who reject Him Will have draughts Of boiling fluids, And a Penalty grievous, Because they did reject Him" (10:4). Sounding like Job's friend who explains that the innocent never perish and the upright are never cut off (Job 4:7), the Quran says:

> Say: "Think ye, if The Punishment of Allah Comes to you, Whether suddenly or openly, Will any be destroyed Except those who do wrong? We send the Messengers Only to give good news And to warn: so those Who believe and mend (Their lives)—upon them Shall be no fear, Nor shall they grieve. But those who reject Our signs—them Shall punishment touch, For that they ceased not From transgressing." (6:47–49)

The problem for Muslims today is similar to that of the priestly and apocalyptic writers of the Hebrew Scriptures who tried to explain exile and foreign domination of "the chosen people." If Allah is powerful and in control of history, and if you and your people are doing well, then your blessings confirm your God, your faith, your sacred text, and your religion. Not doing well creates a crisis and requires an explanation. The military and political successes that resulted in creation of an Islamic Empire far greater than the Roman Empire at its zenith, for example, are understood to be consequences of fidelity to Allah and confirmation of Islam. How then does one explain why an Islamic Empire declined and gave way to domination by imperial, capitalistic, Western, and mostly "Christian" nations? The logical answer reflects a seemingly universal priestly logic: historical prominence gave way to crisis because Muslims had been unfaithful to Allah, the Prophet, and the Quran.

John Esposito captures the essence of this explanation in his description of Hamas, an offshoot of the Palestinian Brotherhood created during the Palestinian *intifada* (uprising) in 1987:

> As its charter states, Hamas "found itself at a time when Islam disappeared from life. Thus, rules were broken, concepts were vilified, values changed, and evil people took control; oppression and darkness prevailed, cowards became tigers; homelands were invaded, people were scattered. . . . When Islam is absent from the arena, everything changes." From this perspective, Israel's occupation is seen as a punishment from God for deviations from Islam. Thus, independence, civil and political rights, dignity, and development will all be achieved only by a return to Islam, a re-Islamization of Palestinian Muslim society.[2]

Numerous passages in the Quran reinforce the view that historical failures are consequences of religious failures. Military victories are attributed to faithfulness, and military setbacks are linked to doubt. Faithlessness is severely punished, and purifying religion is a prerequisite for future success:

> The Hypocrites will be In the lowest depths Of the Fire; no helper Wilt thou find for them—Except for those who repent, Mend (their life), hold fast To Allah, and *purify their religion* As in Allah's sight; if so They will be (numbered) With the Believers.

And soon will Allah Grant to the Believers A reward of immense value. (4:145–146, emphasis added)

In the context of present historical crises, many passages in the Quran could *reasonably be interpreted* to justify violence against "unfaithful" Muslims and other "disbelievers," including Christians and Jews.

THREATS OF HELL LINKED TO POOR CONDUCT OR USED TO MOTIVATE POSITIVE BEHAVIOR

The Quran encourages Muslims to work for justice and live by what are understood to be ethical standards. They are to use their wealth to serve Allah's purposes and give alms to the poor (2:264–265), help orphans (4:8), and loan money without interest (2:245; 3:130). They are to refrain from taking bribes (5:106) and from gambling or using alcohol (2:219). They are not to kill themselves or covet what Allah has bestowed on others (4:29, 32), or "take life—which Allah Has made sacred—except For a just cause" (17:33), or engage in infanticide because of fear of poverty (17:31), or commit adultery (17:32), or engage in homosexual acts (7:81).

The situation of women in Islamic countries varies greatly depending as much or more on cultural patterns and tradition as on the Quran. Within the Quran itself, women are accorded rights that were at the time denied to most Jewish and Christian women. Women are not property to be inherited (4:19), like men they can earn fortunes (4:32), and they have rights to inherit property (4:7). They also have the right to initiate divorce and have certain protections if divorced by men (2:228). On the other hand, menstruating women are "A hurt and a pollution" (2:222); If "ye have been in contact with women," you are unsuitable for prayer (4:43); women are considered war booty (33:50); the testimony of two women is the equivalent of one man's testimony (4:11); believing women must be modest in order not to arouse the sexual passions of men and must lower their gaze, not display their beauty, lower veils over their bosoms, and not strike their feet so as to call attention to hidden ornaments (24:31); the wives of the Prophet are instructed to "stay quietly in Your houses" (33:33); women found guilty of "lewdness" are to be confined to their houses until death (4:15); and although in marriage "They [women] are your garments And ye [men] are their garments" (2:187), the Quran is clear that "men are in charge of women" (4:33).³ Indeed, men are the presumed audience in all of these verses in the Quran that address the role, conduct, and rights of women.

Muslims are to "believe and do deeds of righteousness" (4:57). They are to show kindness to "parents, kinsfolk, Orphans, those in need, Neighbors who are near, Neighbors who are strangers, The Companion by your side, The wayfarer (ye meet)," and captives of war (4:36). They are to do deeds of charity, justice, and conciliation (4:114), and "strive As in a race in all virtues" (5:48).

These and other positive and negative admonitions in the Quran are backed up with threats of God's punishing violence. People must walk "the straight way" because "Those whose (portion) is not wrath" are those "who go not astray" (1:6–7). The Quran, like the Hebrew Scriptures, says abundant rainfall is a conditional blessing (Lev 26:3–4; Quran 11:52). The directive to help orphans (4:8) is followed by threats: "Those who unjustly Eat up the property Of orphans, eat up A Fire into their own Bodies: they will soon Be enduring a blazing Fire!" (4:10). People who "took usury" receive a "grievous punishment" (4:161). Admonitions to use wealth wisely and not to kill oneself (4:29) are followed by warnings: "If any do that In rancour and injustice—Soon shall We cast them Into the Fire: and easy It is for Allah" (4:30). Muslims are not to steal; those who do can be punished severely: "As to the thief, Male or female, Cut off his or her hands: A punishment by way Of example, from Allah, For their crime: And Allah is Exalted in Power, Full of Wisdom" (5:38). "The woman and the man Guilty of adultery or fornication—Flog each of them With a hundred stripes: Let not compassion move you" (24:3).

The essence of spiritual violence is the use of divine threats to condition human behavior. Spiritual violence lies at the heart of hundreds of passages in the Quran but is encapsulated in these words:

> Those who reject Our Signs, We shall soon Cast into the Fire; As often as their skins Are roasted through, We shall change them For fresh skins. That they may taste The Penalty: for Allah is Exalted in Power, Wise. But those who believe And do deeds of righteousness, We shall soon admit to Gardens, With rivers flowing beneath—Their eternal home; Therein shall they have Companions pure and holy: We shall admit them To shades, cool and ever deepening. (4:56–57)

PARALLEL STORIES OF GOD'S PUNISHING VIOLENCE

Muhammad is positioned in the Quran as the most important and final of many prophets or "warners" sent by God to encourage proper belief and right conduct. Allah destroyed many nations and peoples prior to the Arabs in Muhammad's time because they failed to heed God's commands and warnings:

> See they not how many Of those before them We did destroy?—Generations We had established On the earth, in strength Such as We have not given to you—for whom We poured out rain From the skies in abundance, And gave (fertile) streams Flowing beneath their (feet): Yet for their sins We destroyed them. And raised in their wake Fresh generations (To succeed them). (6:6)

> How many towns have We Destroyed (for their sins)? Our punishment took them On a sudden by night Or while they slept For their afternoon rest. When (thus) Our punishment Took them, no cry Did they utter but this: "Indeed we did wrong." (7:4–5)

The Quran repeats or adapts many stories from the Hebrew Scriptures. "Abraham was not a Jew Nor yet a Christian; But he was true in Faith, And bowed his will to Allah's, (Which is Islam), And he joined not gods with Allah" (3:67). Israel's covenant with Allah is retold. "And remember We took A covenant from the Children Of Israel (to this effect): Worship none but Allah; Treat with kindness Your parents and kindred, And orphans and those in need; Speak fair to the people; Be steadfast in prayer; And practice regular charity. Then did ye turn back, Except a few among you, And ye backslide (even now)" (2:83). The consequences of disobedience and backsliding are severe (2:94–96).

Many stories in the Quran with biblical parallels underscore the punishing or liberating violence of God. Moses strikes terror into the people with his magic (7:116), and with Allah's help he confronts and defeats Pharaoh:

> And Pharaoh proclaimed Among his people, saying: "O my people! Does not The dominion of Egypt Belong to me, (witness) These streams flowing Underneath my (palace)? What! See ye not then? Am I not better Than this (Moses), who Is a contemptible wretch And can scarcely Express himself clearly? Then why are not Gold bracelets bestowed On him, or (why) Come (not) with him Angels accompanying him In procession?" Thus did he make Fools of his people. And they obeyed him: Truly were they a people Rebellious (against Allah). When at length they Angered Us, We exacted Retribution from them, and We drowned them all. And We made them (A people) of the Past And an Example To later ages. (43:51–56)

Noah is one of Allah's many rejected warners. "We overwhelmed In the Flood those Who rejected Our Signs. Then see what was the end Of those who were warned (But heeded not)!" (10:73). It similarly tells how Allah saved Lot and his family (except his disobedient wife) while destroying Lot's foes. "When Our decree issued, We turned (the cities) Upside down, and rained down On them brim-stones Hard as baked clay, Spread, layer on layer" (11:82). David's defeat of Goliath is presented as Allah's doing and is cast in specifically religious terms:

> When they advanced To meet Goliath and his forces, They prayed: "Our Lord! Pour out constancy on us And make our steps firm: Help us against those That reject faith." By Allah's will, They routed them: And David slew Goliath: And Allah gave him Power and wisdom And taught him Whatever (else) He willed. And had not Allah Checked one set of people By means of another, The earth would indeed Be full of mischief: But Allah is full of bounty To all the worlds. (2:250–251)

VIOLENCE AND WARFARE AGAINST RELIGIOUS OTHERS AND ENEMIES

In the post-September 11 world, many people are concerned that Islam not be painted as a religion prone to intolerance and violence. One can find many texts that urge Muslims to work for justice, help the needy, and be compassionate toward others. Although it may be troubling to me and to others that some of the "ethical mandates" in the Quran are less than ethical (e.g., denunciation of homosexuals, flogging of adulterers, and cutting off the hands of thieves), and that such mandates come with the threat of violent sanctions, there is no denying that many Muslims see the heart of Islam being the multi-faceted struggle to build a community that reflects what is understood to be Allah's will. Muslims and others seeking to counter charges that Islam is prone to intolerance and violence can point to the ethical behavior and strong community evident in the lives of most Muslims. They can also cite a number of passages from the Quran urging tolerance and restraint:

> Let there be no compulsion In religion: Truth stands out Clear from Error: whoever Rejects Evil and believes in Allah hath

grasped The most trustworthy Handhold, that never breaks. (2:256)

Fight in the cause of Allah Those who fight you, But do not transgress limits; For Allah loveth not transgressors. (2:190)

Say ye: "We believe in Allah, and The revelation given to us, and To Abraham, Ismail, Isaac, Jacob, And the descendents (children Of Jacob) and that given to Moses and Jesus and that given To (all) Prophets from their Lord: We make no difference Between one and another of them: And we bow to Allah (in Islam)." (2:136)

Passages such as these that urge tolerance and respect diversity are unfortunately overwhelmed by others in the Quran, including those within the same sura. The verse urging Muslims to fight within limits is consistent with Just War theory. It is followed, however, by these words: "And slay them Wherever ye catch them, And turn them out From where they have Turned you out; For tumult and oppression Are worse than slaughter" (2:191). Elsewhere this sentiment is repeated word for word (2:217). The statement "we make no difference between one and another" seems to be a statement of religious tolerance. "There be no compulsion in religion" also implies respect for religious diversity and for belief without coercion—but the verse that follows reads:

Allah is the Protector Of those who have faith: From the depths of darkness He will lead them forth Into light. Of those Who reject faith the patrons Are the Evil Ones: from light They will lead them forth into the depths of darkness. They will be Companions Of the fire, to dwell therein (Forever). (2:257)

The problem of Islam and violence is not limited to incompatible texts but is rooted in the overwhelming preponderance of passages in the Quran that legitimate violence, warfare, and intolerance. Violence in service to Allah is both justified and mandated by Allah or Muhammad under the sanction of divine threat. "Fighting is prescribed

Upon you, and ye dislike it. But it is possible That ye dislike a thing Which is good for you, And that ye love a thing Which is bad for you. But Allah knoweth, And ye know not" (2:216). Violence against the other is reinforced by tidy divisions between good (us) and evil (them). "Those who believe Fight in the cause of Allah, And those who reject Faith Fight in the cause of Evil" (4:76).

Christians, Jews, and "pagans" often receive harsh treatment in the Quran, including justified violence against them:

But when the forbidden months Are past, then fight and slay The Pagans wherever ye find them, And seize them, beleaguer them, And lie in wait for them In every stratagem (of war); But if they repent, And establish regular prayers And practice regular charity, Then open the way for them; For Allah is Oft-Forgiving, Most Merciful. (9:5)

Fight those who believe not In Allah nor the Last Day, Nor hold that forbidden Which hath been forbidden By Allah and His Messenger, Nor acknowledge the Religion Of Truth, from among The People of the Book, Until they pay the Jizyah [poll tax levied on non-Muslims] With willing submission, And feel themselves subdued. (9:29)

Of those who refuse to pay for war "We shall say: 'Taste ye the Penalty Of the Scorching Fire'" (3:181). Conversely those who "believe And adopt exile, And fight for the Faith In the cause of Allah, As well as those Who give (them) asylum And aid" will have their sins forgiven (8:74). Refusing to fight is a grave sin, and "Allah Has full knowledge of those Who do wrong" (2:246). Fighting brings rewards. Refusing to fight brings disgrace and ultimately a brutal punishment from Allah:

Of those who answered The call of Allah And the Messenger, Even after being wounded, those who do right And refrain from wrong Have a great reward—Men said to them: "A great army is gathering Against you, so fear them": But it (only) increased Their Faith; they said: "For us Allah sufficeth, And He is the best Disposer of affairs." And they returned With Grace and Bounty From Allah; no harm Ever touched them. . . . It is only the Evil One That suggests to you The fear of his votaries: Be not afraid Of them, but fear Me, if ye have Faith." (3:172–175)

Muslims are to "Worship none but Allah" (2:83), and they are ordered not to associate with unbelievers. "Let not the Believers Take for friends or helpers Unbelievers rather than Believers: if any do that, In nothing will there be help From Allah" (3:28). Muslims are "the best Of Peoples, evolved for mankind, Enjoining what is right, Forbidding what is wrong." Most other "People of the Book . . . Are perverted transgressors" (3:110). Expressing sentiments similar to Ezra, who forced Jews to divorce their foreign wives in order to keep the holy seed of Israel pure and to mitigate Yahweh's wrath, the Quran says: "Take not into your intimacy Those outside your ranks: They will not fail To corrupt you. They only desire your ruin" (3:118). "O ye who believe! Take not the Jews And the Christians For your friends and protectors. . . . Verily Allah guideth not A people unjust" (5:51).

It is an obligation to wage war against disbelievers (3:141), to remain steadfast amid apparent defeat (3:146), to pray for victory over unbelievers (3:147), and to trust that Allah gives "A reward in this world" and "the excellent reward of the Hereafter" to those who fight (3:148). "Allah hath full knowledge Of your enemies: Allah is enough for a Protector, And Allah is enough of a Helper" (4:45). Muslims can have confidence "that for those Who oppose Allah and His Messenger, Is the Fire of Hell" (9:63). They are urged to "slacken not In following up the enemy" (4:104) and to fight with the assurance of Allah's help. "Fight in Allah's cause" and "rouse the believers" because Allah is "strongest in might" and may "restrain the fury Of the Unbelievers" (4:84).

Those who grow weary are urged to continue fighting with promises of the Hereafter. "'Our Lord! Why hast Thou ordered us To fight? Wouldst Thou not Grant us respite To our (natural) term, Near (enough)?' Say: 'Short Is the enjoyment of this world: The Hereafter is the best for those who do right' " (4:77). Unbelievers are to be pursued and killed:

> They but wish that ye Should reject Faith, As they do, and thus be On the same footing (as they): So take not friends From their ranks Until they flee In the way of Allah (From what is forbidden). But if they turn renegades, Seize them and slay them. (4:89)

Many passages reinforce the same sentiment. "And fight them [unbelievers] on Until there is no more Tumult or oppression, And there prevails Justice and faith in Allah" (8:39). "If ye gain mastery Over them in war, Disperse, with them, those Who follow them, That they may remember" (8:57). Another translation of the same verse reads, "If thou comest on them in the war, deal with them so as to strike fear in those who are behind them, that haply they may remember."[4] "It is not fitting For a Prophet That he should have Prisoners of war until He hath thoroughly subdued The land" (8:67), or otherwise translated, "It is not for any Prophet to have captives until he hath made slaughter in the land."[5] "O Prophet! Strive against the disbelievers and the hypocrites! Be harsh with them. Their ultimate abode is hell, a hapless Journey's end" (9:73).[6] "Against them make ready Your strength to the utmost Of your power, including Steeds of war, to strike terror Into (the hearts of) the enemies" (8:60). After the slaughter and after striking terror into the enemy, believers are to enjoy the spoils of war. "But (now) enjoy what ye took In war, lawful and good" (8:69).

Those who fight against Allah and Muhammad deserve severe punishment in this world and the next:

> The punishment of those Who wage war against Allah And His Messenger, and strive With might and main For mischief through the land Is: execution, or crucifixion, Or the cutting

off of hands And feet from opposite sides, Or exile from the land: That is their disgrace In this world, and A heavy punishment is theirs In the Hereafter. (5:33)

Therefore, when ye meet The Unbelievers (in fight), Smite at their necks; At length, when ye have Thoroughly subdued them, Bind a bond Firmly (on them). . . . But those who are slain In the way of Allah—He will never let Their deeds be lost. Soon will He guide them And improve their condition, And admit them to The Garden which He Has announced for them. (47:4–6)

PARADISE PROMISES

Just as the book of Daniel encouraged resistance to Antiochus with the assurance of resurrection, so too the Quran promises heavenly rewards to those who fight and die. "And say not of those Who are slain in the way Of Allah: 'They are dead.' Nay, they are living, Though ye perceive (it) not" (2:154). "And if they are slain, or die, In the way of Allah, Forgiveness and mercy From Allah are far better Than all they could amass. And if ye die, or are slain, Lo! It is unto Allah That ye are brought together" (3:157–158). "Think not of those Who are slain in Allah's way As dead. Nay, they live, Finding their sustenance In the presence of their Lord" (3:169).

Those who have left their homes, And were driven out therefrom, And suffered harm in My Cause, And fought and were slain—Verily, I will blot out From their iniquities, And admit them into Gardens With rivers flowing beneath—A reward from the Presence Of Allah, and from His Presence Is the best of rewards. (3:195)

Risking death in service to Allah is logical given the folly of this world and the promise of a better hereafter (14:3; 16:107; 42:36). "What is the life of this world But play and amusement? But best is the Home In the Hereafter, for those Who are righteous, Will ye not then understand?" (6:32). "As to the dead, Allah will Raise them up; then will they Be returned unto Him" (6:36). What "is the matter with you . . . [that] ye cling heavily to the earth? Do ye prefer the life Of this world to the Hereafter? But little comfort Of this life, as compared With the Hereafter" (9:38). "Allah hath purchased of the Believers Their persons and their goods; For theirs (in return) Is the Garden (of Paradise): They fight in His Cause, And slay and are slain" (9:111).

There is even the promise, according to some interpretations, that there will be virgins waiting for those who die in service to Allah:

> As to the Righteous (They will be) in A position of Security. Among Gardens and Springs; Dressed in fine silk And in rich brocade, They will face each other; Moreover, We shall Join them to Companions [*hur*] With beautiful, big, And lustrous eyes. There they call For every kind of fruit In peace and security; Nor will they there Taste Death, except the first Death; and He will preserve Them from the Penalty Of the Blazing Fire—As a Bounty from thy Lord! That will be The supreme achievement. (44:51–57)

If one scholar is correct that *hur* has been translated virgin but in early Arabic actually meant white raisin (a delicacy in the ancient Near East), then there may be many disappointed men who have fought and died in service to Allah.[7]

A mother of a Palestinian suicide bomber has her son's portrait hanging next to gold-framed verses from the Quran. She says of her son, who detonated himself in a Jerusalem pizzeria, killing himself and 15 others (including 6 children) and wounding 130: "I think someone put into [my son's] head that this [suicide bombing] was the way to go to paradise."[8] Abdulaziz bin Abdallah al Sheikh, the leading Islamic scholar in Saudi Arabia, says suicide bombings are "illegitimate and have nothing to do with jihad in the cause of God."[9] Sheikh Ahmed Yassin, the spiritual leader of Hamas, disagrees. Although he believes suicide bombers should target Israeli military and government leaders and not civilians, he says, "Everyone who dies in war or is killed by the enemy is considered a martyr."[10] The interpretations of both sheikhs are reasonable in light of the Quran. Although the Quran prohibits suicide, it requires warfare when Islam is under attack, and it lifts up the promise of paradise for soldiers and martyrs.

GOD AS HOLY WARRIOR

Promises of paradise and threats of punishments for disobedience are not the only motivating factors by which the Quran encourages human violence and warfare. The Quran presents Allah as an all-powerful holy warrior. David slew Goliath "By Allah's will" (2:251). Those who fight on behalf of Allah defeat armies "Twice their number" because "Allah doth support With His Aid whom He pleaseth. In this is a warning For such as have eyes to see" (3:14). "O Prophet! Rouse the Believers To the fight. If there are Twenty amongst you, patient And persevering, they will Vanquish two hundred: if a hundred, They will vanquish a thousand of the Unbelievers" (8:65). "Allah had helped you At Badr, when ye were A contemptible little force; Then fear Allah; thus May ye show your gratitude" (3:123). Muslims can remain firm in battle: "Even if The enemy should rush here on you in hot haste, Your Lord would help you With five thousand angels Making a terrific onslaught" (3:125). There is no victory except from Allah (3:126; 8:10). "Fight them, and Allah will Punish them by your hands, Cover them with shame, Help you (to victory) over them, Heal the breasts of Believers" (9:14). "Allah will Certainly aid those who Aid His (cause)—for verily Allah is Full of Strength" (22:40). He promises "speedy victory . . . To the Believers" (61:13).

> Remember thy Lord inspired The angels (with the message): "I am with you: give Firmness to the Believers: I will instill terror Into the hearts of Unbelievers: Smite ye above the necks And smite all their Finger tips off them. This because they contended Against Allah and His Messenger: If any contend against Allah And His Messenger, Allah Is strict in punishment. Thus

(will it be said): 'Taste ye Then of the (punishment): For those who resist Allah, Is the penalty of the Fire.' O ye who believe! When ye meet The Unbelievers In hostile array, Never turn your backs To them. If any do turn his back To them on such a day—Unless it be in a stratagem Of war, or to retreat To a troop (of his own)—He draws on himself The wrath of Allah, And his abode is Hell—An evil refuge (indeed)! It is not ye who Slew them; it was Allah." (8:12–17)

Assuredly Allah did help you In many battlefields. . . . Allah did pour His calm On the Messenger and on the Believers, And sent down forces which ye Saw not: He punished The Unbelievers: thus doth He Reward those without Faith. (9: 25–26)

FODDER FOR EXTREMISTS

It is sobering that the Islamic terrorists who flew airplanes into the World Trade Towers and the Pentagon could have had any of many dozens of verses from the Quran in their hearts or on their lips. In light of the collective weight of violence-legitimating passages in the Quran, it seems to me that it is less than forthcoming to speak of Islam being hijacked by extremists.[11] Passages, considered individually or collectively, could *reasonably be interpreted* to justify or even require violence, terrorism, and war against enemies in service to Allah or in pursuit of "Islamic justice." To the many passages already cited, I add several that may have helped motivate Islamic extremists as they flew airplanes into the World Trade Towers and the Pentagon in service to Allah:

Did the people of the towns Feel Secure against the coming Of Our wrath by night While they were asleep? Or else did they feel Secure against its coming In broad daylight while they Played about (carefree)? Did they then feel secure Against the Plan of Allah?—But no one can feel Secure from the Plan Of Allah, except those (Doomed) to ruin. (7:97–99)

Say to the desert Arabs Who lagged behind: "Ye Shall be summoned (to fight) Against a people given to Vehement war: then shall ye Fight, or they shall submit. Then if you show obedience, Allah will grant you A goodly reward, but if Ye turn back as ye Did before, He will punish You with a grievous Penalty." (48:16)

Say: "Can you expect for us (Any fate) other than one Of two glorious things—(Martyrdom or victory)? But we can expect for you Either that Allah will send His punishment from Himself, Or by our hands." Let not their wealth Nor their (following in) sons Dazzle thee: in reality Allah's plan is to punish them with these things in this life, And that their souls may perish In their (very) denial of Allah. (9:52, 55)

Those who love the life Of this world more than The Hereafter, who hinder (men) From the Path of Allah And seek therein something crooked: They are astray By a long distance. (14:3)

Do those who devise Evil (plots) feel secure That Allah will not cause The earth to swallow them up, Or that the Wrath will not Seize them from directions They little perceive? Or that He may not Call them to account In the midst of their goings To and fro, without a chance Of their frustrating Him? (16:45–46)

So We sent against them A furious Wind through days Of disaster, that We might Give them a taste Of a Penalty of humiliation In this Life; but the Penalty Of the Hereafter will be More humiliating still: And they will find No help. (41:16)

Then watch thou For the Day That the sky will Bring forth a kind Of smoke (or mist) Plainly visible, Enveloping the people: This will be a Penalty Grievous. (44:10–11)

CONCLUSION

The Hebrew Scriptures, the Christian New Testament, and the Quran contain stories urging compassionate living, social justice, and ethical conduct. The collective weight of *all* passages in these texts that advocate ethical behavior or present evidence of a loving, compassionate God cannot, however, overcome the violent images and expectations of God that overwhelm these "sacred" texts. God's violence or human violence justified in service to God is sometimes understood to be the principal means to justice in, or at the end of, history. At other times, ethical conduct is urged under the threat of God's punishing violence. God's violence is at times so pervasive, unpredictable, vindictive, or destructive that it reflects a deep and troubling pathology. In such cases, we can say that if human beings acted as God does or as God tells them to act, then they would rightfully be considered certifiably insane. Religious violence prevalent among the followers of monotheistic faith traditions is not primarily a problem of believers distorting their "sacred" texts. It is, rather, a problem rooted in the violence-of-God traditions that lie at the heart of these "sacred" texts.

NOTES

1. Except as otherwise noted, citations from the Quran are from 'Abdullah Yusuf 'Ali (translator), *The Meaning of The Holy Qur'an* (Lahore, India: Muhammad Ashraf, 1937–1938; 10th ed.; Beltsville, Md.: Amana Pubs., 1999); online: http://mukhtar.home.mindspring.com.

2. John L. Esposito, *Unholy War: Terror in the Name of Islam* (New York: Oxford University Press, 2002), 96.

3. This verse is translated by Marmaduke William Pickthall, *Glorious Quran: Final Revelation from God* (London: A. A. Knopf, 1930; Chicago: Iqra' Book Center, n.d.).

4. Ibid.

5. Ibid.

6. Ibid.

7. This is the view of Christoph Luxenberg, a scholar of ancient Semitic languages. See Alexander Still, "Radical Theories Offered on Origins of the Qur'an," *Minneapolis Star Tribune* (Mar. 10, 2002).

8. Joyce M. Davis, "The Mind of a Suicide Bomber," *St. Paul Pioneer Press* (Apr. 7, 2002).

9. Ibid.

10. Ibid.

11. Esposito, *Unholy War,* 22.

7. Room for Doubt?

The Church's tradition . . . reserves the designation of inspired texts to the canonical books of the Old and New Testaments, since these are inspired by the Holy Spirit. Taking up this tradition, the Dogmatic Constitution on Divine Revelation of the Second Vatican Council states: "For Holy Mother Church, relying on the faith of the apostolic Testaments, whole and entire, with all their parts, on the grounds that, written under the inspiration of the Holy Spirit . . . they have God as their author, and have been handed on as such to the Church herself." These books "firmly, faithfully, and without error, teach that truth which God, for the sake of our salvation, wished to see confided to the Sacred Scriptures." (Vatican's Offices of the Congregation for the Doctrine of the Faith)[1]

This Quran is not such As can be produced By other than Allah; On the contrary it is A confirmation of (revelations) That went before it, And a fuller explanation Of the Book wherein There is no doubt—From the Lord of the Worlds. Or do they say, "He forged it"? Say: "Bring then A *Surah* like unto

95

it, And call (to your aid) Anyone you can, Besides Allah, if it be
Ye speak the truth!" (10:37–38)

—⌐⌐—

I BEGIN THIS CHAPTER WITH FOUR STATEMENTS I hold to be
true in light of the analysis in previous chapters. First, the Hebrew
Scriptures, the Christian New Testament, and the Quran contain
strong admonitions not to doubt. Second, fundamentalists are disliked
by many mainstream Jews, Christians, and Muslims, but all three bodies share a similar aversion to challenging the authority of their re-
spective "sacred" texts. Third, our unwillingness honestly to confront
the violence-of-God traditions at the heart of our "sacred" texts puts
the world in grave peril. Finally, doubt is vital to our prospects for
survival. Religious and political certitude are killing us because they
encourage intolerance and violence.

The focus of chapter 7 is on doubt or the absence of doubt in
Islam. Chapter 8 examines what it might mean for us to be saved by
enemies. Finally, chapter 9 explores how we are saved by doubt.
Doubting the authority of "sacred texts" that legitimate violence is
an essential act of faithfulness.

I DOUBT IT

The Hebrew Scriptures, the Christian New Testament, and the
Quran say doubt is a very bad thing. The priestly and prophetic story
line says that if you believe, you will do well, and if you disbelieve,
you face dire consequences. The book of Numbers, for example, says
that when "the people fail to believe that Yahweh can drive out the
Canaanites for them, God condemns the entire older generation—
including Moses, Aaron, and Miriam—to die in the wilderness."[2]
The New Testament says Jesus is the only way to God, and that
people who believe and are baptized will be saved. Others will be
damned. The failure of Jews to believe in Jesus, according to the
Gospel writers, led God to destroy the Jews and the temple in

Jerusalem. John addressed a crisis of faith in his community that resulted from unfulfilled promises and expectations surrounding Jesus' "imminent" return by telling the story of "doubting Thomas" (20:24–29). John retrojected the problem of doubt back into Jesus' lifetime to suggest that Jesus anticipated the problem of doubt that plagued John's community some seventy years after Jesus died. John's message is clear: there is no need to doubt God's (John's) promises.

Muslims are instructed not to doubt under threat of divine wrath. The Quran claims to be "a Book Of Exalted power," and it warns that people "who reject the Message . . . Are not hidden from Us" (41:41). Those who "dispute Concerning Allah," "on them Is Wrath, and for them Will be a Penalty Terrible" (42:16). The Quran "verily . . . is Truth Of assured certainty" (69:51).

One obstacle standing in the way of a serious challenge to the violence-of-God traditions in the Bible and the Quran is that influential authorities say these texts were written by God. Using words from one of my children's favorite card games, "I doubt it." I doubt that God orders us to kill disobedient children, requires that we stone to death people who gather sticks on the Sabbath, sends she-bears out to maul boys who insult a prophet, or rejoices at reducing the chosen people to cannibalism, as the Hebrew Scriptures claim. I doubt that God zapped a couple who withheld a portion of their land sale, that Jesus will cast those who don't bear good fruit into a fire, or that love of enemies can be reconciled with the Lamb who will return to oversee the destruction of much of humanity at the end time, as the New Testament writers claim. I doubt that those who fail to assist orphans will soon be enduring a blazing fire, that Allah punishes disobedience by causing droughts, or that Allah wants thieves to have their hands cut off, as the Quran says.

Attributing every word of the Quran directly to Allah or claiming God or the Holy Spirit as the author of biblical texts leaves little latitude for scriptural challenges, new revelations, and new interpretations that are desperately needed if the world is to pull back from the deadly precipice of violent destruction rooted in our distorted images of a violent God. The writers of the Bible and the Quran are often treated as if they absorbed God's Image, God's Self, and God's Essence with the efficiency of sponges absorbing water. It would be more accurate to say that if God's revelation is like water that God hopes will be absorbed into the life of the world, then these writers receive this water more like asphalt than sponges.

SANCTIFYING VIOLENCE

Jews, Christians, and Muslims encourage violence because they refuse to fully challenge the authority of "sacred texts" that overflow with violent images of God and stories justifying human violence in God's name. Male presumptions of violent power have been projected onto God and have triumphed over reason, history, and faith. As the ecofeminist Christian writer Ivone Gebara writes, "'macho' men continue to be regarded as the most important mediators of the sacred."[3] Purging violence–of–God traditions from the Bible and the Quran threatens to undermine them altogether. Christian rituals and hymns are so saturated in violent images of God (often masquerading as themes of liberation or atonement) that those who challenge them are considered heretics. Purging Christianity of violent images of God would also force Christians to take nonviolent power and the radical nonviolence of Jesus seriously, something few seem willing to do.

Scores of violence-justifying passages cited in Chapter 6 indicate that Muslims face significant challenges in coming to terms with the violence that is featured so centrally in the Quran. A difficult issue is whether Muslims can find, or have an interest in finding, a way to grapple forthrightly with the violence-of-God traditions at the heart of the Quran when the Quran itself says it "is Truth Of assured certainty" and cannot be challenged because it is God's direct revelation. Depending on one's perspective, Muslims either face unique obstacles to challenging scriptural authority or they are uniquely gifted because they have no need of doing so. Muslims are more apt to memorize the Quran than they are to analyze it and use scholarly tools similar to those employed by Christian and Jewish scholars. John Esposito writes:

> Islam's doctrine of revelation (*wahy*) also contrasts with that of modern biblical criticism. Both the form and the content, as well as the message and the actual words, of revelation are attributed to an external source, God. Muhammad is merely an instrument or a conduit. He is neither author nor editor of the Quran, but God's intermediary.[4]

Methodologies that might shed light on the violence-of-God traditions in light of Muhammad's life or in the context of how, where, and why the Quran took shape are rejected out of hand as un-Islamic. Thus the director of the Islamic Center of Minnesota wrote in response to an article that challenged traditional views of Islam's origins:

> [We accept] the trustworthiness of the messenger, the sensibility and consistency of the message as well as the quality of its preservation and transmission. Muslims have no problems with any of these elements underlying their faith. They do not need to distill the core of the message from a garbled set of messages transmitted to them over the ages. The methodologies that may be necessary for scholars of other faiths are by definition unnecessary when evaluating Islam.[5]

DOWNPLAYING THE VIOLENCE

Standard portraits of Islam's origins ignore, downplay, sanitize, or justify the violence-of-God traditions in the Quran. Most Muslim and non-Muslim scholars of Islam report that in 610 C.E. an illiterate Arab businessman who ritually retired to a cave just outside Mecca for prayer and fasting began receiving revelations from God. At the time Mecca was a thriving mercantile city and had for many decades been a central worship cite for pagan pilgrims. Elite traders had grown rich in the context of worship and trade but the culture itself was one of violence, vendetta, tribalism, and greed.

In this setting God (Allah) spoke to Muhammad and to the Arabs. Allah gave them a "sacred text" in their own language and a prophet of their own, to help them break the brutal pattern of life in Arabia, where "one tribe fought another, in a murderous cycle of vendetta and counter-vendetta." At the time there was, according to Karen Armstrong, "a spiritual restlessness in Mecca and throughout the peninsula. Arabs knew that Judaism and Christianity, which were practiced in the Byzantine and Persian empires, were more sophisticated than their own pagan traditions."[6]

The center of pagan religious life at the time of Muhammad was, according to the traditional view, the *Kabah* (Kaaba), a cube-shaped shrine at the heart of Mecca. The *Kabah* was a gathering place for pilgrims who "would circle the shrine seven times, following the direction of the sun around the earth; kiss the Black Stone embedded in the wall of the Kabah, which was probably a meteorite that had once hurtled to the ground, linking the site to the heavenly world."[7] The shrine was officially dedicated to a Nabatean deity, Hubal, but was also home to hundreds of idols, perhaps one for each day of the year. Some Arabs "had come to believe that the High God of their pantheon, al-Lah (whose name simply meant 'the God'), was the deity worshipped by the Jews and the Christians, but he had sent the Arabs no prophet and no scripture in their own language."[8] Muhammad was that prophet, Arabic was the language, and the Quran was the book. "The Quran was revealed to Muhammad verse by verse, *surah* [chapter] by *surah* during the next twenty-one years, often in response to a crisis or a question that had arisen in the little community of the faithful."[9]

Muhammad's message, according to the traditional portrait, was that Allah required justice, and that Muslims were to submit to Allah and struggle to build a righteous community. Muhammad was the final "warner" or prophet to announce God's intentions, including benefits for obedience and crushing punishments for disobedience. Annemarie Schimmel, in her book *Islam: An Introduction,* writes:

> The first proclamations preached by Muhammad are dominated by one single thought: the nearing of the Day of Judgment. The terrible shock caused by the sudden approach of the Hour, the Day of Reckoning, and the resurrection is heralded by breathless short lines in sonorous rhymed prose. Close is this Hour. In a short while it will knock at the door and will stir up from heedlessness those who are embroiled in worldly affairs and who have forgotten God! . . . Certain trials have to be faced, and finally the unbelievers and sinners will be dragged away by their feet. . . . Later popular piety . . . could never get enough detail of all kinds of chastisement; of terrible pain in the fire; of stinking, hot, or dirty water; of the fruits of poisonous trees; and of various tortures. But Muhammad learned that he was not only sent to threaten and to blame, but also to bring good tidings: every pious man who lives according to God's order will enter Paradise where rivers of milk and honey flow in cool, fragrant gardens and virgin beloveds await him. Women and children too participate in the paradisial bliss.[10]

Another central theme in the standard portrait of Islam's origins is that Muslims established a vast empire because Muhammad and Islam were faithful to God's will. The rapid spread of Islam, in other words, proved the claims of Muhammad, the Quran, and Allah. Karen Armstrong describes the rapid spread of Islam and military triumphs during the leadership of Umar ibn al-Khattab (634–44):

> Under Umar's leadership, . . . the Arabs burst into Iraq, Syria and Egypt, achieving a series of astonishing victories. They overcame the Persian army at the Battle of Qadisiyyah (637), which led to the fall of the capital of the Persian Sassanids at Ctesiphon. As soon as they had the manpower, Muslims would

thus be able to occupy the whole of the Persian Empire. They encountered stiffer resistance in the Byzantine Empire. . . . Nevertheless, the Muslims were victorious at the Battle of Yarmuk (636) in northern Palestine, conquered Jerusalem in 638, and controlled the whole of Syria, Palestine and Egypt by 641. The Muslim armies went on to seize the North African coast as far as Cyrenaica. Just twenty years after the Battle of Badr [Muslims inflicted a dramatic military defeat on the Meccans at the Battle of Badr in 624], the Arabs found themselves in possession of a sizeable empire. This expansion continued. A century after the Prophet's death, the Islamic Empire extended from the Pyrenees to the Himalayas. It seemed yet another miracle and sign of God's favour. Before the coming of Islam, the Arabs had been a despised outgroup; but in a remarkably short space of time they had inflicted major defeats upon two world empires. The experience of conquest enhanced their sense that something tremendous had happened to them. . . . Their success also endorsed the message of the Quran, which had asserted that a correctly guided society must prosper because it was in tune with God's laws. Look what had happened once they had surrendered to God's will! Where Christians discerned God's hand in apparent failure and defeat, when Jesus died on the cross, Muslims experienced political success as sacramental and as a revelation of the divine presence in their lives.[11]

This traditional story line, which links military success to faithfulness, and idealizes and justifies redemptive violence, is repeated in most introductory texts on Islam. Karen Armstrong writes, "when the Muslims had established their great empire, Islamic law would give a religious interpretation of this conquest, dividing the world into the Dar al-Islam (the House of Islam), which was in perpetual conflict with the Dar al-Harb (the House of War)." "But," she continues, "in practice the Muslims accepted that they had reached the limits of their expansion. . . . The Quran does not sanctify warfare. It develops the notion of a just war of self-defence [*sic*] to protect decent values, but condemns killing and aggression."[12] "Muhammad's use of warfare in general," John Esposito writes, "was alien neither to Arab custom nor to that of the Hebrew prophets. Both believed that God had sanctioned battle with the enemies of the Lord."[13] Esposito hereby justifies the violence-of-God tradition within Islam because such a tradition also dominated the Hebrew Scriptures. An alternative is to condemn both.

Violence justifying portraits of Islam's rise have a dangerous political afterlife, a point seemingly made but ignored by Esposito:

> In 624 at Badr, near Medina, Muslim forces, though greatly outnumbered, defeated the Meccan army. For Muslims, then and now, the battle of Badr has special significance. It was the first and a most decisive victory for the forces of monotheism over those of polytheism, for the army of God over the followers of ignorance and unbelief. God had sanctioned and assisted His soldiers (Quran 3:123, 8:42ff) in victory. Quranic witness to divine guidance and intervention made Badr a sacred symbol, and it has been used throughout Muslim history, as evidenced most recently in the 1973 Egyptian-Israeli war, whose Egyptian code name was "Operation Badr."[14]

Esposito doesn't ponder the implications of why "Operation Badr" led to a crushing defeat for Muslims.

A prominent subtheme within the widely accepted portrait of Islam's origins is that all the details of Muhammad's life, including his rulings that make up a good deal of the Muslim legal codes, were known definitively because the stories of the prophet (*hadith*) were faithfully transmitted by his early followers.

UNWANTED ALTERNATIVES

The violence-of-God tradition is central to the Quran and it is justified within traditional portraits of the rise and spread of Islam. The pressing question is whether and on what basis this tradition can be challenged. A number of scholars dispute the traditional portrait and the subtheme appended to it. If their findings are taken seriously, then claims of Islam and the Quran are open to debate, including the presumption that superior violence proves that God is God.

First, in her book *Meccan Trade and the Rise of Islam* Patricia Crone writes that Mecca wasn't an important trade site during the time of Muhammad and the Quran's supposed origins.[15] Crone says the sources of the rise of Islam are wrong in one or more fundamental respects and that it is far more likely that Islam took shape far from Mecca in a monotheistic setting. "Muhammad's career [was] in northwest Arabia" and "yet everything is supposed to have happened much further south, in [Mecca]."[16] This information would not be particularly troubling except that if Mecca was not a trading city and not a religious center of "idol worship," then the Quran isn't absolute truth and the product of God's direct dictation to Muhammad. Many Muslims consider such information to be as unwelcome as a hole in a bucket. It is useless because it makes the whole bucket useless.

Second, it is likely that Islam *followed* rather than *preceded* Arab military victories and political expansion. Karen Armstrong, a strong Western voice for the official tradition, inadvertently strengthens the view that conquest may have preceded Islam. When "the Arabs burst out of Arabia they were not impelled by the ferocious power of 'Islam,'" she writes. "Western people often assume that Islam is a violent, militaristic faith which imposed itself on its subject peoples at sword-point. This is an inaccurate interpretation of the Muslim wars of expansion," she continues. "*There was nothing religious about these campaigns,* and Umar did not believe that he had a divine mandate to conquer the world. The objective of Umar and his warriors," Armstrong reports, "was entirely pragmatic: they wanted plunder and a common activity that would preserve the unity of the *ummah* [community]."[17]

Islam may have evolved in the aftermath of Arab expansionism instead of preceding it. A tradition justifying conquest and emphasizing the central role of Muhammad and Mecca may have taken shape later. If this is true, then the idea that military victory and imperial expansion are fruits of faithfulness could be confronted.

A third challenge to traditional portraits of Islam is related to how much or how little we know about Muhammad. The first biography of Muhammad was written a hundred years after the events they supposedly portray. It may be problematic, therefore, to base Islam's legal code on stories about the prophet (*hadith*) because such stories are unreliable. Annemarie Schimmel writes:

> A "scientific" critique of *hadith* in the western sense is suspect for most pious Muslims, and besides, it is considered irrelevant, as Muhammad, being a true prophet, could have foreseen and foretold many future developments and given much advice which western investigators might see as a foreign import. There are, however, some modernist schools in Islam which reject the authenticity of *hadith,* and reject it in toto.[18]

DOES IT MATTER?

Critical scholarship can challenge violence-of-God traditions in the Hebrew Scriptures because it makes clear that human writers over many hundreds of years shared ideas on how God or the gods interacted with the world. We see the gradual development of a one-God tradition, the evolution of God's power, the influence of different writers, the crisis of exile, the frustrations growing out of unfulfilled promises, and the near constant projections of abusive, violent power onto God.

The situation is similar in Christianity. The New Testament offers evidence of different writers and oral traditions that offer conflicting and incompatible portraits of Jesus. Scholars can wrestle with competing claims and can trace different streams within the Gospel accounts. We get glimpses of the historical Jesus and snapshots of diverse belief systems traceable to different early church communities. We see evidence of conflicts over leadership, fights over the proper roles of women, competing explanations for historical problems, and different expectations about what God was doing in light of historical difficulties. We have scholarly tools that show that Jesus neither claimed to be God nor to be the only way to God, as John's Gospel suggests in its many "I am" statements attributed to Jesus.[19]

The brief look at Islam in light of such scholarship indicates that if Muslims were willing to travel this road it would likely lead far away from traditional views concerning the origins of Islam, the nature of the Quran, and the role of Muhammad. That is why critical scholarship of this kind has almost no place in Islamic studies. Depending on perspective, one person thinks "insights" from such scholarship might help transform Islam, and another thinks "distortions" and "heresies" embedded in such scholarship are dangerous and damaging.

If one assumes, as most Muslims do, that the Quran is literally God's *final* word to humanity, then challenging the violence-of-God traditions discussed in Chapter 6 becomes far less likely than if one sees human authors and interests invading the text. Muslim rejection of the scholarly insights described above is not meant to suggest that Islam is monolithic in perspective. There is tremendous diversity *within the acceptable boundaries* of Islamic discourse. Annemarie Schimmel writes that the "Koran is the basis for the entire life, be it the regulation of religious duties or problems of art. Hence it is natural that a vast range of interpretations and commentaries should have developed in the course of the centuries."[20] There are "fundamentalist circles" for whom "the Law is considered to be the 'spiritual regulator' of the community," and Sufi "mystics" who have "striven to reach a more profound understanding of the Divine word" by searching for "a deeper meaning [that] lies behind the words of the text and that one has to penetrate to the true core."[21] There are Sunni Muslims who try to stick to Muhammad's words, actions, and customs, and Shiite groups who stress "the esoteric meaning of the Koranic word."[22] "According to Islamic doctrine, the style of the Koran is inimitable and of superhuman beauty and power. Not only does the text contain the solutions for all problems that arise in the world," Annemarie Schimmel writes, "but there are also unknown Divine mysteries hidden in the sequence of its verses and in the arrangements of its very letters."[23]

Central to all these groups and perspectives is the Quran itself. But what of the violence? How will it be challenged and by whom? The Arab poet Adonis accuses Islamic clerics of "past-ism," the tendency to cling to what is known and fear that which is new. "We live in a culture that doesn't leave a space for questions . . . ," Adonis says. "It [the culture] knows all the answers in advance. Even God has nothing left to say."[24] Shafi A. Khaled rejects questions concerning the origin of the Quran: "Muslims don't need help interpreting the Qur'an."[25] Perhaps not, but they are needed as partners in a global struggle for justice and against violence.

Muslims may challenge the pervasive violence at the heart of the world's life and Muslim life in ways other than a direct confrontation with their "sacred" text. Farid Esack, a Muslim liberation theologian, says Muslims must contextualize the Quran if they are to find meaning. "Belief in the eternal relevance of the Qur'an," he writes, "is not the same as belief in a text which is timeless and spaceless."

> There is a theological and historical basis for justifying a contextual approach to the Qur'an itself and the role of people in elaborating its meaning. This approach has enabled many a progressive Islamist in South Africa to engage the apartheid regime meaningfully and in solidarity with the religious Other. They have done so despite the qur'anic warning to those of faith against "taking the Christians and Jews as their *awliya'* (friends/allies/supporters)." (5:51)[26]

The common struggle against apartheid, in other words, required a more inclusive reading of the Quran. Badshah Khan, one of the greatest nonviolent activists in the history of the world, took a similar approach when he linked the struggle for justice to Gandhi's nonviolent methods (see chapter 9). It may be that violence will show itself to be such a destructive, ineffective, and dangerous response to injustice that it will prompt a re-imaging of both God's power and human power. The search for alternatives to violence in a wounded world could well be the common bond that brings together Jews, Christians, Muslims, and many other people of diverse faiths to create a world that better reflects the compassion many believers attribute to God.

CONCLUSION

Jews, Christians, and Muslims must address the problem of violence and "sacred" text if we are to have any reasonable hope for an alternative future. A world being destroyed by violence, much of it done with justifying reference to God and "sacred" text, is a world in desperate need of new understandings of divine and human power. The futility of violence and resiliency of injustice requires us to unleash our imaginations in order to move beyond religious certainties into unfamiliar terrain where patriarchal assumptions that dominate "sacred" texts and political life are challenged in light of historical need and human experience. As Ivone Gebara writes:

> The patriarchal world always made distinctions between the good and the bad, the just and the unjust, and the masculine and the feminine; it always erected clear boundaries around what it pompously judged to be good, just, pure, and perfect. The closing of this century offers us the great challenge of learning to think of ourselves in categories that are no longer oppositional, but rather inclusive.[27]

NOTES

1. The Declaration "Dominus Iesus," from the Offices of the Congregation of the Doctrine of the Faith (August 6, 2000), in the Introduction.

2. Stephen Harris, *Understanding the Bible* (5th ed.; Mountain View, Calif.: Mayfield Publishing Company, 2000), 134.

3. Ivone Gebara, *Longing for Running Water: Ecofeminism and Liberation* (Minneapolis: Augsburg Fortress, 1999), 16.

4. John L. Esposito, *Islam: The Straight Path* (New York: Oxford University Press, 1998), 20–21.

5. Shafi A. Khaled, "Muslims don't need help interpreting the Qur'an," *Minneapolis Star Tribune* (May 12, 2002).

6. Karen Armstrong, *Islam: A Short History* (N.Y.: Random House, 2000), 3.

7. Ibid., 11.

8. Ibid., 3.

9. Ibid., 4.

10. Annemarie Schimmel, *Islam: An Introduction* (Albany, N.Y.: State University Press of New York, 1992), 12-13.

11. Armstrong, *Islam: A Short History,* 27, 29.

12. Ibid., 30.

13. Esposito, *Islam: The Straight Path,* 15.

14. Ibid., 9.

15. Patricia Crone, *Meccan Trade and the Rise of Islam* (Cambridge, U.K.: Cambridge University Press, 1987).

16. Ibid., 196-99.

17. Armstrong, *Islam: A Short History,* 29–30 (emphasis added).

18. Schimmel, *Islam: An Introduction,* 53.

19. Robert W. Funk et al., *The Five Gospels: What Did Jesus Really Say?* (Santa Rosa, Calif.: Polebridge Press, 1993).

20. Schimmel, *Islam: An Introduction,* 47.

21. Ibid., 48–50.

22. Ibid., 48, 51.

23. Ibid., 30.

24. Quoted in the *New York Times* (July 13, 2002), A15.

25. *Minneapolis Star Tribune* (May 12, 2002).

26. Farid Esack, *Qur'an, Liberation and Pluralism: An Islamic Perspective on Interreligious Solidarity Against Oppression* (Oxford, U.K.: Oneworld Publications, 1997), 49.

27. Gebara, *Longing for Running Water,* 108.

8. Saved by Enemies

[This is] the gift our enemy may be able to bring us: *to see aspects of ourselves that we cannot discover any other way than through our enemies.* Our friends seldom tell us these things; they are our friends precisely because they are able to overlook or ignore this part of us. The enemy is thus not merely a hurdle to be leaped on the way to God. The enemy *can be* the way to God. We cannot come to terms with our shadow except through our enemies, for we have almost no other access to those unacceptable parts of ourselves that need redeeming except through the mirror that our enemies hold up to us. This then is another, more intimate reason for loving our enemies: . . . we may not be whole people without them [emphasis in original].[1]

—Walter Wink

Why do you see the speck in your neighbor's eye, but do not notice the log in your own eye? Or how can you say to your

neighbor, "Friend, let me take out the speck in your eye," when
you yourself do not see the log in your own eye? You hyp-
ocrite, first take the log out of your own eye, and then you will
see clearly to take the speck out of your neighbor's eye. (Luke
6:41–42)

[The hated Samaritan] went to him and bandaged his wounds,
having poured oil and wine on them. Then he put him on his
own animal, brought him to an inn, and took care of him.
(Luke 10:34)

—Jesus

All that was required of them was a primitive patriotism which
could be appealed to whenever it was necessary to make them
accept longer working hours or shorter rations. And even
when they became discontented, as they sometimes did, their
discontent led nowhere, because, being without general ideas,
they could only focus it on petty specific grievances. The larger
evils invariably escaped their notice.

—George Orwell, *1984*

MANY PASSAGES IN THE BIBLE AND THE QURAN divide the world
neatly between good and evil. There are insiders who know what
God wants and outsiders who don't. In fidelity to God, "we" can and
must strive to defeat outsiders (enemies). "We" is a self-designation
that places us on the side of good and of God, thus allowing us to act
with confidence that God will reward our efforts and punish or help
us to defeat our adversaries. "Our nation," George W. Bush proclaims,
"is chosen by God and commissioned by history to be a model for
the world."[2] By extension, U.S. violence is an instrument of God's
will. "If we have to use force," Madeleine Albright asserts, "it is
because we are America! We are the indispensable nation!"[3]

Good versus evil, insider versus outsider, we versus they, those who know God versus those who don't—these opposing pairs are elements in a political and religious worldview that discourages self-reflection and impedes our sight. They lead to an escalating spiral of violence. We magnify our enemy's faults but diminish our own short-comings. We can't or won't entertain the idea that our enemies some-times see us better than we see ourselves, and that the things they see are important for them and us to know.

Among the radical claims of Jesus, none is more shocking and more important to our prospect for building a world without reli-giously sanctified violence than his claim that we are saved by our enemies. Muslim terrorists and other enemies are not going to bind up our wounds like the hated Samaritan in Jesus' parable. They may, however, offer insights into ourselves that we ignore to the world's and our own peril. The present chapter explores what being saved by enemies might mean in the context of the terrorist attacks of Sep-tember 11, 2001.

SELECTIVE HISTORY

My Lenten discipline in 2002 was to assess Jesus' prospects if he were to show up in the United States post-September 11. I concluded that—because of his likely conflict with authorities, nonviolent actions, teachings on love of enemies, and warnings against the futil-ity of violence—Jesus would have been killed in a matter of weeks, days, or hours.

The terrorist attacks of September 11 carried out by Muslim ex-tremists were monumental crimes against humanity. They spawned shock and outrage. Logic and emotion dictated that we hate and not love Osama bin Laden or his followers; the idea that they may some-how hold the key to our salvation and healing seemed absurd. Jesus, therefore, was pushed aside as U.S. citizens hoisted mountains of U.S. flags and listened to an avalanche of violent, patriotic rhetoric that discouraged any authentic probe of why the attacks occurred. Columnist Michael Kelly wrote in the *Washington Post* that the

"American pacifists are on the side of future mass murderers of Americans. They are objectively pro-terrorist. . . . That is the pacifist's position, and it is evil."[4] Ann Coulter, a nationally syndicated columnist, expressed similar sentiments in her address to the 2002 Christian Action Conference: "When contemplating college liberals, you really regret once again that John Walker [a U.S. citizen captured while fighting for the Taliban in Afghanistan] is not getting the death penalty. We need to execute people like John Walker in order to physically intimidate liberals, by making them realize that they can be killed too. Otherwise," she continues, "they will turn out to be outright traitors."[5]

In this political climate, most Christians choose to ignore Jesus in favor of retaliatory violence, and most citizens eagerly embraced the explanations of leaders who said we were attacked because of our basic goodness and the base evil of our attackers. They hate us because we are good. We love freedom, democracy, and pluralism. They incarnate evil, are motivated by hate, and are at war with goodness. We, therefore, can rightfully hate them, hunt them down, and kill them in a permanent war against terrorism. God, of course, is on our side.

There was little if any room for self-reflection in this closed-circle explanation. There was no need to analyze why—if the United States is as good as we claim—we were hated by so many, or to explore what Osama bin Laden meant when he said that the "real targets [of September 11] were America's icons of military and economic power" [the Pentagon and the World Trade Towers].[6] There was also no awareness that although 84 percent of U.S. adults say they are Christian, the United States is arguably the most militarized country in the world, spending nearly $400 billion a year (about $750,000 a minute) on its military. U.S. forces train approximately 100,000 foreign soldiers annually in at least 150 institutions within the United States and in 180 countries around the world.[7] Ironically, Christians raised the specter of Islam and violence while they ignored Jesus and overwhelmingly supported the U.S.-directed, open-ended war against terrorism.

These oversights might be slightly amusing except that our ignorance has deadly consequences. The terrorist attacks of September 11
and the violent reprisals that followed demonstrate how important it
is that we see the log in our own eye. When giving public talks, I
sometimes ask several questions in an effort to bring a piece of the
log into focus. Typical exchanges go something like this:

JNP: What happened on September 11, 2001? *Response:* The terrorist attacks. *JNP:* Very good. Now, who can tell me what happened
on September 11, 1973? *Response:* Silence. *JNP:* On September 11,
1973, a U.S.-orchestrated coup in Chile overthrew Salvador Allende,
the democratically elected president, and replaced him with a brutal
military dictatorship headed by General Augusto Pinochet. There is
thorough documentation that the coup was carried out by the CIA
under orders of President Nixon and with personal guidance from
Secretary of State Henry Kissinger.[8] Kissinger ordered the assassina-
tion (carried out) of the chief of the Chilean Army because he up-
held the Chilean constitution. In the aftermath of the coup, the
U.S.-backed dictatorship killed or disappeared thousands of Chilean
workers, students, and progressive religious. It also, with U.S. assistance, set up an international death squad linking secret police forces
throughout Latin America. Operating under the code name Operation
Condor, it assassinated, abducted, intimidated, and tortured numerous
dissidents. "United States government complicity has been uncovered
at every level of this network."[9]

JNP: What happened on December 7, 1941? *Response:* Pearl
Harbor. *JNP:* Excellent. Who says we don't know history? Now,
who can tell me what happened on December 7, 1975? *Response:* A
long silence with a few wild guesses but no right answer. *JNP:*
December 7, 1975, is a day of infamy and genocide for the people of
East Timor. On this day more than 200,000 people, about one-third
of the island's population, were massacred by Indonesian troops using
U.S. weapons and with explicit approval from U.S. leaders. According
to recently declassified documents, Indonesia's President Suharto met
with President Ford and Secretary of State Kissinger in Jakarta on
the eve of the invasion and told them of his plans to carry out the

slaughter. "We want your understanding if we deem it necessary to take rapid or drastic action," Suharto said. "We will understand," Ford responded, "and we will not press you on the issue. We understand the problem you have and the intentions you have." Kissinger was concerned with logistics, including the efficiency and timing of the slaughter. "It is important that whatever you do succeeds quickly," he said. "We would be able to influence the reaction in America if whatever happens happens after we return."[10] December 7, 1975, was, according to Noam Chomsky, "the worst slaughter relative to population since the Holocaust."[11]

JNP: One final question. How many people died on September 11, 2001? *Response:* Approximately three thousand. *JNP:* Yes and no. That is the estimated death toll from the terrorist attacks at the World Trade Towers and the Pentagon. The events of September 11 and the death toll are almost incomprehensible. We are right to condemn the attacks, right to grieve and mourn the senseless slaughter of innocents, and right to seek justice for those responsible for the attacks. When we ponder the enormity of the death toll that day, however, we should also remember that more civilians were killed in the U.S. bombings of Afghanistan since September 11 than were killed at the World Trade Towers and the Pentagon.[12] We should also ponder another death toll. According to the Food and Agricultural Organization (FAO) of the United Nations, 35,615 children died of hunger on September 11, 2001. We and they are victims of selective history, memory, and outrage. Every senseless death fills and refills a reservoir of hate.

The limited knowledge of history reflected in these interchanges begins to clarify what I mean when I say that we must be saved by our enemies. The examples given—a coup in Chile, genocide in East Timor, enormous death tolls from hunger that are part of daily life in the global economy—illustrate what many, particularly oppressed people, have always known: people suffer and die because U.S. citizens know little about their country's role in the world. Many people hate us, in other words, not because of our goodness, but because of specific grievances rooted in specific U.S. policies.

Having a better handle on why we may be hated, however, doesn't address what it means to say that our enemies hold the key to our own well-being. Here is the link. The most important unlearned lesson of September 11 is that our ignorance is costly to ourselves as well as to others. This means that shallow explanations for the terrorist attacks, explanations that focus on our goodness and the evil nature of our enemies, are dangerous. They provide false comfort without responding to real grievances. The log in our eye is intact: we can't see the causes of the hatred directed toward us, which in turn leaves us less secure than we were before September 11. No matter how many billions of dollars we spend and how many "terrorists" we kill, we will be vulnerable to future terrorist attacks. U.S. military responses to September 11 make us less secure because they offer a simplistic response to complex problems made artificially simple by our genuine myopia. The inevitable result of vilifying enemies and militarizing U.S. foreign policy is that we fill and refill the reservoir of hate that gives rise to terrorism. That is why seeing ourselves through the eyes of our enemies is the key to transformation and to our own salvation.

LISTENING TO AND LEARNING FROM ENEMIES

The nonviolent Buddhist monk Thich Nhat Hanh, when asked what he would say to Osama bin Laden after September 11, said he would listen for a very long time in order to better understand the hate behind the actions. This is good advice despite the protestations of our leaders and many columnists who believe that self-criticism and introspection are treasonous acts condoning or justifying the attacks. Listening to enemies is important because, as Walter Wink said in the quote introducing this chapter, they help us "see aspects of ourselves that we cannot discover any other way than through our enemies." Enemies can be "the way to God" for us; using Jesus' language, they help us see the log in our eye that we refuse to see.

Without any pretense to being thorough, let me briefly describe five key issues brought to light by our enemies, including Osama bin

Laden and others responsible for the terrorist attacks of September 11. How enemies perceive us may not always be entirely accurate, but they undoubtedly contain elements of truth that are important to their well-being and our own. We will either learn from enemies or perish in a mutually destructive, escalating spiral of hatred and violence.

The first lesson we learn from our enemies is that *U.S. policies in the Middle East justifiably generate deep resentments and hatred.* U.S. policies have been driven by two goals: the desire to control Middle Eastern oil supplies and unwavering support for the State of Israel. Two-thirds of the world's known oil reserves are located in the Middle East. The U.S. State Department calls this oil "a stupendous source of strategic power" and "one of the greatest material prizes in history."[13] U.S. oil politics and repression go hand in hand in many parts of the world, including the Middle East; Afghanistan, where the U.S. courted the Taliban in an effort to get permission to build an oil pipeline; and Colombia, where oil interests are secured with the help of paramilitary groups guilty of horrific human rights atrocities.[14] We can no longer afford to ignore connections between gas-guzzling SUV's, repressive oil politics, and bitter resentment against the United States.

Our government is committed to controlling governments in the Middle East that are given only nominal say over the resources within their borders. U.S. influence is often secured through repressive leaders, including dictators like Saddam Hussein (he later became an enemy when he overstepped the line of nominal control), autocratic regimes like the emirs in Kuwait, and the repressive Shah of Iran (overthrown in an anti-U.S. revolution). U.S. support extends to a Taliban-like, radical Muslim extremist government, such as the one in Saudi Arabia, which receives billions of dollars in oil revenues, buys billions of dollars worth of U.S. weapons, and funds terrorists.[15] The militarized State of Israel functions as an unofficial U.S. military base in the region.

The permanent U.S. military presence in Saudi Arabia (where Mecca and other Muslim holy sites are located) and uncritical U.S. support for Israel generate deep resentments and hatred of the

United States among many Muslims. The United States gave Israel more than $18 billion in military assistance between 1990 and 2000 as Israel dramatically expanded settlements in territories it illegally occupies.[16] The pro-Israeli lobby is strong, and it includes many fundamentalist Christians who believe Israel's right to the land is firmly established in the Hebrew Scriptures, and that Israel's existence is a necessary prelude to both the coming of the Antichrist and the Second Coming of Christ.

Many Muslims hold the United States accountable for Israeli atrocities against the Palestinian people. Osama bin Laden's words resonate with many:

> For over half a century, Muslims in Palestine have been slaughtered and assaulted and robbed of their honor and of their property. Their houses have been blasted, their crops destroyed. And the strange thing is that any act on their part to avenge themselves or lift the injustice befalling them causes agitation in the United Nations, which hastens to call an emergency meeting only to convict the victim and to censure the wronged and tyrannized, whose children have been killed and whose crops have been destroyed and whose farms have been pulverized.[17]

The U.S.-led sanctions against Iraq are another source of deep anti-American feeling. According to the United Nations, economic sanctions had killed *1.5 million* Iraqis by 1999,[18] more than 500 times the death toll of September 11. Imagine the horror of duplicating the death toll of September 11 every month into the indefinite future. The brutal sanctions against the people of Iraq are seen as part of a consistent U.S. war against Islamic people and nations. "America and its allies are massacring us in Palestine, Chechnya, Kashmir, and Iraq," Osama bin Laden said. "The Muslims have the right to attack America in reprisal. The September 11 attacks were not targeted at women and children. The real targets were America's icons of military and economic power."[19]

A second lesson we can learn from our enemies is that *corporate-led globalization is bitterly resented by many. It benefits a relatively small segment of humanity, undermines indigenous cultures, erodes democracy, destroys the environment, and is imposed by violence linked to U.S. militarization.* In the quote above, Osama bin Laden said specifically that the World Trade Towers and Pentagon were targeted on September 11 because they are icons of U.S. economic and military power. To help us understand what this means, I comment briefly on several quotes from Thomas Friedman, a popular, arrogant, and articulate spokesperson *for* corporate-led globalization.

Friedman places great faith in the "Electronic Herd and the Supermarkets," by which he means the global system that allows people and groups to scour the world in search of profits by moving money around with the click of a mouse. He admits, however, that globalization is responsible for widening inequalities and that the gap between winners and losers is "staggering."[20] In "a winner-take-all world," Friedman writes, "America, for the moment at least, certainly has the winner-take-a-lot system."[21]

Friedman acknowledges that globalization is a race to the bottom for poor people as national leaders compete with each other to better exploit their people and the environment in order to please "the Herd." "The Supermarkets" "play Syria off against Mexico off against Brazil off against Thailand. Those who perform are rewarded with investment capital from the Supermarkets. Those who don't are left as roadkill on the global investment highway."[22]

On January 1, 1994, the Zapatistas in Chiapas timed their rebellion to correspond to the implementation date of the North American Free Trade Agreement (NAFTA). They did so in order to make a point about globalization's negative impact on indigenous and other poor people in Mexico. With logs firmly blocking our vision, few U.S. citizens have heard of the Zapatistas and fewer still considered that the World Trade Towers were targeted for similar reasons. As icons of U.S. economic power, they are a symbol of a global economy that works well for the superrich but marginalizes many. According to the United Nations, the "three richest people have assets that exceed the combined GDP [Gross Domestic Product] of the 48 least developed countries."[23] It should not surprise us that globalization feeds resentments when the world's richest 225 people have combined incomes greater than those of half of humanity, and nearly three billion people struggle to live on less than $2 a day.[24]

The global economy also distorts democracy. On "the political front, the Golden Straitjacket [policies of the Herd and Supermarkets] narrows the political and economic policy choices of those in power to relatively tight parameters," Friedman writes, so that "political choices get reduced to Pepsi or Coke—to slight nuances of taste."[25] The "Electronic Herd gets to vote in all kinds of countries everyday, but those countries don't get to vote on the Herd's behavior."[26]

> The Electronic Herd and the Supermarkets are fast becoming two of the most intimidating, coercive, intrusive forces in the world today. They leave many people feeling that whatever democracy they have at home, whatever the choices they think they are exercising in their local or national elections, whoever they think they elected to run their societies, are all just illusions—because it is actually larger, distant, faceless markets and herds that are dictating their political lives.[27]

Perhaps most important to understanding why globalization feeds resentment of the United States throughout the Muslim world is its impact on religion and culture. The desire to live a more authentically Islamic life is widespread among many Muslims. It is part of a search to find alternatives to the ideologies and actual practices of capitalism, Marxism, or secular nationalism that have failed to meet the social, economic, religious, and cultural needs of people. Globalization, Friedman writes, "is creating a single marketplace" that can "homogenize consumption simultaneously all over the world." It is "a culturally homogenizing and environment-devouring force" that creates "a real danger that in just a few decades it could wipe out the ecological and cultural diversity that took millions of years of human and biological evolution to produce."[28] "Today, for better or for worse," Friedman acknowledges, "globalization is a means for spreading the fantasy of America around the world."[29] "Culturally speaking, globalization is largely, though not entirely, the spread of Americanization—from Big Macs to iMacs to Mickey Mouse—on a global scale."[30] Friedman doesn't say it, but many Muslims are deeply offended by globalization's export of U.S. culture that glorifies violence, drugs, sexual promiscuity, and disrespect for parents and elders.

With all of these downsides named but dismissed in Friedman's own analysis, it should not surprise us that U.S. militarization is the stick that imposes globalization. "The globalization era," Friedman writes, "may well turn out to be the great age of civil wars" between "winners and losers *within* countries."[31] Friedman refers to the United States as "the ultimate benign hegemon and reluctant enforcer."[32] It can exercise power via its economic might, but it also "has a large standing army, equipped with more aircraft carriers, advanced fighter jets, transport aircraft, and nuclear weapons than ever, so that it can project more power farther than any country in the world. And deeper too."[33]

> Sustainable globalization requires a stable power structure, and no country is more essential for this than the United States. All the Internet and other technologies that Silicon Valley is designing to carry digital voices, videos, and data around the world, all the trade and financial integration it is promoting through its innovations, and all the wealth this is generating, are happening in a world stabilized by a benign superpower, with its capital in Washington, D.C. The fact that no two countries have gone to war since they both got McDonald's is partly due to economic integration, but it is also due to the presence of American power and America's willingness to use that power against those who would threaten the system of globalization—from Iraq to North Korea. The hidden hand of the market will never work without a hidden fist. McDonald's cannot

flourish without McDonnell Douglas, the designer of the U.S. Air Force F-15. And the hidden fist that keeps the world safe for Silicon Valley's technologies to flourish is called the U.S. Army, Air Force, Navy, and Marine Corps. And these fighting forces and institutions are paid for by American taxpayer dollars.[34]

A third lesson pressed upon us by how our enemies see and experience us is that *the United States is a leading terrorist state.* The fact that this charge is surprising to most Americans is part of the problem. I pointed out previously that following the attacks of September 11, a British writer described the U.S. Army School of the Americas as "a terrorist training camp" run by the United States for "the past 55 years."[35] I also described how the United States, following the establishment of the Pinochet dictatorship in Chile, helped establish an international death squad to track down "subversives." One of the great ironies of September 11 and the war against terrorism that followed is that the United States helped recruit and train Islamic terrorists from throughout the Middle East because they were useful in our nation's "holy war" against the Soviet Union. We trained Muslim extremists in Pakistan and Afghanistan at the same time we trained the Nicaraguan contras in terrorist tactics, helped the Salvadoran government terrorize its citizens, and worked with death squads in Guatemala and Honduras.[36]

Johan Galtung, perhaps the best-known international peace educator in the world, looked at the United States as a terrorist nation in a different light following the September 11 terrorist attacks. Galtung is concerned that terrorism be consistently condemned in all its manifestations. This means recognizing that there is a "dominant, mainstream discourse" about terrorism that links it to "non-state actors," such as al-Qaida. This discourse is predictably silent about the problem of "state terrorism." Non-state terrorists are those who "have bombs but no airforce" [or who turn civilian planes into bombs] while state terrorists "have both bombs and air force."[37] There is, in other words, terrorism from above and terrorism from below.

Terrorism from below is directed against governments or states as persons or institutions, and of course to bring about political change. Obviously, most governments, and the United Nations as a trade union of governments, are against terrorism from below because, like secession, it affects vital government interests. . . . State terrorism [terrorism from above] as a military tactic also uses surprise and focuses on killing civilians to force capitulation. This is a major theme in modern warfare, indeed used by the US/UK air forces in their terror bombing of Germany and Japan 1940–45. In the campaign against Yugoslavia March–June 1999 remarkably few military targets were destroyed whereas the killing of civilians and destruction of Serbian infra-structure (factories, power, transportation/communication, schools and hospitals) was extensive.[38]

Galtung points out that in terms of actual death and destruction, non-state terrorists can not begin to catch up with the United States. Although non-state and state terror are organized in different ways, "terrorism is terrorism whether from below or from above."[39] Because non-state terror is fed by "an ocean of hate," responding to non-state terror with state terror only escalates the spiral of violence.[40]

A fourth lesson we learn from our enemies, as well as some of our friends, is that *U.S. arrogance in international affairs feeds resentment of the United States.* In the past several years, the U.S. has unilaterally withdrawn from the Kyoto environmental accords aimed at reducing global warming; refused to support the Comprehensive Nuclear Test Ban Treaty and to sign an International Land Mines Treaty; undermined international efforts to curb the sale of small weapons; refused to ratify a treaty for the creation of a permanent International Criminal Court; blocked U.N. efforts to sanction Israel for brutal violence against Palestinians; pulled out of the Anti-Ballistic Missile Treaty (ABM); moved forward on a missile defense system and the militarization of space in opposition to the stated wishes of nearly every country in the world; and undermined international efforts to provide significantly greater development assistance to so-called

Third World nations. If arrogance breeds contempt, then it is little wonder that U.S. unilateral policies that place it above international law are generating a bumper crop of hatred and resentment.

Finally, we learn from our friends and our enemies that *the greatest challenge facing the world today is to make all communities livable.* Developing countries, according to U.N. estimates, could achieve and maintain "universal access to basic education for all, basic health care for all, reproductive health care for all women, adequate food for all, and safe water and sanitation for all" at a cost of approximately 40 billion additional dollars a year. "This is less than 4 percent of the combined wealth of the 225 richest people in the world."[41] Powerful U.S. groups that benefit from militarization have literally capitalized on post-September 11 fears. As a result, U.S. military spending in 2003 approached $400 billion, not counting billions more spent on home land security. The tragedy is that many of these expenditures make us less, rather than more, secure. As a "warning from 100 Nobel Prize Winners" states:

> The most powerful danger in the coming years will stem not from the irrational acts of states or individuals but from the legitimate demands of the world's dispossessed. Of these poor and disenfranchised, the majority live a marginal existence in equatorial climates. Global warming, not of their making but originating with the wealthy few, will affect their fragile ecologies most. Their situation will be desperate and manifestly unjust. It cannot be expected, therefore, that in all cases they will be content to await the beneficence of the rich. If then we permit the devastating power of modern weaponry to spread through this combustible human landscape, we invite a conflagration that can engulf both rich and poor. The only hope for the future lies in cooperative international action, legitimized by democracy. It is time to turn our backs on the unilateral search for security, in which we seek shelter behind walls. Instead, we must persist in the quest for united action to counter both global warming and a weaponized world.[42]

It is clear from the above analysis that not seeing the logs in our own eyes is costly for ourselves and others. Salvation and God's favor can no longer be understood as defeat of enemies, as much of the Bible and the Quran suggests. Among salvation's prominent meanings are healing and wholeness for individuals, communities, and the world itself. Vilifying enemies and militarizing conflicts legitimated by appeals to "sacred" texts escalate a spiral of violence. In this sense, as Jesus suggested, we truly are saved by our enemies. Because our "sacred" texts legitimate violence, we must also be saved by doubt.

NOTES

1. Walter Wink, *Engaging the Powers: Discernment and Resistance in a World of Domination* (Minneapolis: Fortress, 1992), 273.

2. Quoted in Colman McCarthy, *I'd Rather Teach Peace* (Maryknoll, N.Y.: Orbis Books, 2002), 71.

3. Ibid.

4. Cited by Rose Marie Berger, "Beyond Warmongers and Peaceniks," online, *Sojonet* (Feb. 6, 2002), a service of *Sojourners magazine.*

5. Quoted in *Sojonet: Sojomail* (Feb. 13, 2002), online, via *Sojourners.*

6. John L. Esposito, *Unholy War: Terror in the Name of Islam* (New York: Oxford University Press, 2002), 22.

7. Lora Lumpe et al., "Executive Summary" of "U.S. Foreign Military Training: Global Reach, Global Power, and Oversight Issues," online journal, *Foreign Policy in Focus: A Think Tank without Walls* (May 2002).

8. Christopher Hitchens, "The Case against Henry Kissinger, Part Two: Crimes against Humanity," *Harper's Magazine* (Mar. 2001), 50.

9. Ibid.

10. Quoted in the *Arms Trade Resource Center Update* (Dec. 20, 2001), 5, online, www.worldpolicy.org.

11. Ibid.

12. Marc W. Herold, "A Dossier on Civilian Victims of United States' Aerial Bombing of Afghanistan: A Comprehensive Accounting," on-line, http://www.medialens.org/articles_2002/mh_civilian_victims.html.

13. *Z Magazine* (Jan. 1991), 55.

14. "The Ties That Bind: Colombia and Military-Paramilitary Links," *Human Rights Watch,* vol. 12, No. 1 (B) (Feb. 2000), online, www.hrw.org/reports/2000/colombia.

15. See Esposito, *Unholy War.*

16. "Friend to Friend to Foe: How U.S. Arms Transfers to Israel Come Back to Haunt Both Allies," by Jonathan Reingold in an article from the *Arms Trade Resource Center,* online, www.worldpolicy.org (Apr. 18, 2002).

17. Esposito, *Unholy War,* 23.

18. See Project Ploughshares website.

19. Esposito, *Unholy War,* 22.

20. Ibid., 250.

21. Thomas L. Friedman, *The Lexus and the Olive Tree: Understanding Globalization* (New York: Farrar, Straus and Giroux, 1999), 304.

22. Ibid., 214.

23. Chuck Collins et al., *Shifting Fortunes: The Perils of the Growing American Wealth Gap* (Boston: United for a Fair Economy, 1999), 18.

24. Ibid.

25. Friedman, *The Lexus,* 87–88.

26. Ibid., 163.

27. Ibid., 142.

28. Ibid., 221.

29. Ibid., 235.

30. Ibid., 8.

31. Ibid., 212, emphasis in original.

32. Ibid., 375.

33. Ibid., 304.

34. Ibid., 373.

35. George Monbiot, "Backyard Terrorism," *The Guardian* (Oct. 30, 2001). For information on a nonviolent movement to close the School of the Americas, see online www.soaw.org.

36. See Jack Nelson-Pallmeyer, *School of Assassins: Guns, Greed, and Globalization* (Maryknoll: Orbis Books, 2001).

37. Johan Galtung, "September 11, 2001: Diagnosis, Prognosis, Therapy," online, www.peace.ca/September11byjohangaltung.htm.

38. Ibid., 2

39. Ibid.

40. Ibid.

41. Collins, *Shifting Fortunes,* 18.

42. Editorial in *World Watch Magazine,* May/June, 2002, 2.

9. Saved by Doubt

Power is of two kinds. One is dominated by the fear of punishment, and the other by the arts of love. Power based on love is a thousand times more effective and permanent than the one derived from fear of punishment.

—Mohandas K. Gandhi

I believe he [Badshah Khan] offers the world, and particularly Islamic countries, a way out of the violence that has convulsed the Middle East during the last few decades. Khan is the greatest living exponent of nonviolence in the world. As a devout Muslim, his life shows a face of Islam which non-Islamic countries seldom see. Muslims themselves seem to know little of the potential for nonviolent action inherent in the wisdom of Islam. Khan's example proves that within the scope of Islam exists a noble alternative to violence.

—Eknath Easwaran[1]

THE WIDESPREAD ACCEPTANCE of the violence-of-God traditions within the Bible and the Quran, and the broad embrace of violence as a tactic to resolve historical grievances—both are killing us. The most tragic and enduring legacy of these "sacred" texts is that they distort the nature of both divine and human power. Coercive, punishing, violent conceptions of God and power that have their origins in the minds, fantasies, and experiences of men cripple our imaginations and dominate the political, economic, and religious landscape of our world. History shows that we court disaster when we legitimate them with references to the authority of "sacred" scriptures.

The good news is that there is an alternative conception of power rooted in love, and it is, as Gandhi says, effective. Gandhi's experiments in truth revealed that one instrument of effective power is active nonviolence.[2] If we are to be saved from the spiral of violence that threatens us, then we must have sufficient doubt to challenge the authority of the Bible and the Quran that offer distorted images of God and wrongfully associate divine and human power with superior violence and defeat of enemies. We will be saved by our enemies and by our doubt, or we will not be saved at all.

IN DEFENSE OF DOUBT

People are reluctant to challenge the violence-of-God traditions in their "sacred" texts. Some are afraid that doubting the authority of scripture may undermine their faith. Religion is supposed to be a *firm foundation* in an otherwise insecure world, not another reason for insecurity. That is why, in response to rapid change in the modern world, there has been a resurgent fundamentalism within many religions, including Judaism, Christianity, and Islam. Others fear that challenging "sacred" texts will erode confidence in religion and will thereby undercut a principal source of ethical guidance in a world that is increasingly secular and seems to be fraying due to the absence of ethics and morality. Other believers want or need a violent, punishing God. Only a powerful, violent God is deemed capable of defeating enemies, overcoming death, fulfilling heavenly promises, and delivering justice, including rewards for insiders and punishments for outsiders, within or at the end of history.

Doubt of many kinds is a necessary response to a world being torn apart by violence, political and economic arrogance, and religious certitude rooted in "sacred" texts. Although reluctance to doubt may be understandable, it stands in the way of discernment that is necessary if religion is going to help move the world away from the precipice of violent destruction. The reasons against doubt, as noted above, are problematic or overstated for many reasons, three to be explored here.

First, our faith journeys would continue, albeit on a different pathway, even if we set aside our "sacred" texts or the violence-of-God traditions within them. Human beings seem to be spiritual by nature. I believe all religious people are theologians in that they try to make sense out of their lives and out of historical events in light of the sacred or God. As Ivone Gebara writes:

> The search for God is a path we never succeed in leaving behind. All generations walk it in their own ways, often without so much as pronouncing its name. It accompanies us throughout our lives. It is part of our questioning the meaning of life, a questioning that is phrased in a thousand and one ways and that appears and reappears in all cultures and challenges all individuals. In the last analysis, questions about God are questions about ourselves: about the fact of being alive, of being here, of being confronted by countless situations and questions.[3]

People today, like those who penned the Bible and the Quran, are capable of both compelling insights and horrific distortions of God, history, faith, and life. The key point is that religion, with or without "sacred" text, is and always will be a part of the human quest for meaning, at least for most of us.

Second, people who fear that doubting "sacred" texts means losing the ethical guidance of the Bible and the Quran should consider that many people who specifically deny or doubt God's existence behave at least as ethically and morally as those who claim to be guided by these texts. If we take religiously justified violence or certitude out of the equation, many conflicts become less rather than more volatile. Based on the overwhelming violence at the heart of the Bible and the Quran, I conclude that Jews, Christians, and Muslims do reasonably well in terms of compassionate, just, ethical, and moral living. They do so, however, *in spite of much of what is in their "sacred" texts.*

Most of us don't need admonitions and threats from God and "sacred" text to be convinced that it is wrong to murder or exploit others, and that it is right to help orphans and to treat others as we would like to be treated. These and other moral and ethical impulses are part of an enormous bank of wisdom born out of human experience. They will not disappear because we challenge violence-of-God traditions that are imbedded in these texts. Conversely, most believers don't kill disobedient children or stone to death people who work on the Sabbath even though God in the Bible instructs them to do so and threatens to punish them if they don't. Most don't slaughter enemies and claim booty as divine gift even though parts of the Bible and the Quran encourage these despicable acts.

The basic sense of justice and decency in spite of sacred text was evident in the Day of Prayer for Peace attended by religious leaders from many faith traditions, in response to the terrorist attacks of September 11 and the violence that followed. The Day of Prayer for Peace was convened by Pope John Paul II on January 24, 2002, at Assisi, "in the shadow of Saint Francis, . . . who witnessed to nonviolence, to peace with all people, and to harmony of all creation."[4] Participants representing Judaism, Christianity, Islam, Shintoism, Sikhism, Hinduism, Buddhism, Jainism, Confucianism, Zoroastrianism, and Traditional African religions declared: "Violence never again! War never again! Terrorism never again! In God's name, may all religions bring upon earth justice and peace, forgiveness, life and love." They issued a collective statement, the "Decalogue of Assisi for Peace," with the following points:

1. We commit ourselves to proclaiming our firm conviction that violence and terrorism are incompatible with the authentic spirit of religion, and, as we condemn every recourse to violence and war in the name of God or of religion, we commit ourselves to doing everything possible to eliminate the root causes of terrorism.

2. We commit ourselves to educating people to mutual respect and esteem, in order to help bring about a peaceful and fraternal coexistence between people of different ethnic groups, cultures, and religions.

3. We commit ourselves to fostering the culture of dialogue. . . .

4. We commit ourselves to defending the right of everyone to live a decent life. . . .

5. We commit ourselves to frank and patient dialogue, refusing to consider our differences as an insurmountable barrier, but recognizing instead that to encounter the diversity of others can become an opportunity for greater reciprocal understanding.

6. We commit ourselves to forgiving one another for past and present errors and prejudices, and to supporting one another in a common effort both to overcome selfishness and arrogance, hatred and violence, and to learn from the past that peace without justice is no true peace.

7. We commit ourselves to taking the side of the poor and the helpless. . . .

8. We commit ourselves to taking up the cry of those who refuse to be resigned to violence and evil, and we . . . desire to make every effort possible to offer the men and women of our time real hope for justice and peace.

9. We commit ourselves to encouraging all efforts to promote friendship between peoples, for we are convinced that, in the absence of solidarity and understanding between peoples, technological progress exposes the world to a growing risk of destruction and death.

10. We commit ourselves to urging leaders of nations to make every effort to create and consolidate, on the national and international levels, a world of solidarity and peace based on justice.

These statements express a compelling vision of people of different faiths working together to build a world of diversity, nonviolence, justice, and peace. In my view, however, it is doubtful that most people will seriously consider this vision until the countervailing violence-of-God traditions imbedded in their "sacred" texts are formally acknowledged and rejected.

A third reason that fears of questioning the "authority" or "sacredness" of the Bible and the Quran are exaggerated is that there are alternative ways of reading these texts. Many Christians and Jews have spiritualized violent passages in the Psalms and other texts as a way of sidestepping or denying the full weight of biblical violence. Gandhi did much the same in relation to violence-justifying passages in the *Bhagavad Gita* (see below). There is, however, a simpler and in my view more compelling alternative. What if Jews, Christians, and Muslims were to view the Bible and Quran as products of human beings who offered their views on how history intersects with the divine? What if we treated the voices behind these texts respectfully but refused to let them serve as blind guides? What if we saw these ancestors in the faith as both insightful and fallible and thus capable of both revealing and distorting God?

This approach would encourage us to take our own faith journeys seriously. It would allow us learn from the ideas and experiences of our predecessors in faith without falling into the grave temptation of assuming that answers to important life questions are embedded in the past instead of unfolding in the mystery of the present and future. It acknowledges that our spiritual ancestors passed on to us in the Bible and the Quran their sometimes insightful, often distorted, view of God, life, history, and faith, including the overwhelming human tendency to project violent power onto God. The best they can offer us is the possibility of gleaning something of value from both their insights and their distortions.

The key point is that we do not need to throw our "sacred" texts away in order to come to terms with their violence. In fact, we can learn as much or more from their distortions of God, God's power, and human power as we can from their positive insights. Accepting human authorship of the Bible and the Quran and the inevitable distortions of God that accompany all human efforts to interpret human experience as religious experience would open up many possibilities. It would allow us to see the legacy of abusive men's power in the Bible and Quran, including how male conceptions of punishing, coercive violence are projected onto God and used to justify human violence against women and outsiders. This could be a basis to reflect on similar dynamics at play in our world, where men, violence, and religion are links in a strong chain holding the world captive to violence. We could examine explanations for historical catastrophes, expectations of God's power, and justifications for human violence in the Bible and the Quran in light of present injustices and similarly distorted views of history, violence, and power today.

The problem with this alternative approach or way of reading "sacred" texts is that it is unthinkable for many Jews and Christians and would be considered scandalous by many Muslims. It seems to me, however, that whatever method or pathway Jews, Christians, and Muslims choose, they must effectively challenge the violence-of-God traditions at the heart of the Bible and the Quran. Doing so is an essential component of faithfulness as we seek to create an alternative future consistent with God's compassion.

Moving the world away from the precipice of violent destruction, however, requires more. We can be saved by doubt in three critical areas. First, doubt can allow us to challenge the worldview into which we have been deeply socialized, to see ourselves through the eyes of our enemies, and to embrace Jesus' radical claim that *salvation is not defeat of enemies, but that we are in fact saved by our enemies.* Second, people—whether religious or not—must doubt the efficacy of violence and embrace alternative forms of nonviolent power. Finally, Christians need to embrace, and others may learn from, the "doubting Jesus" who rejected, challenged, or revolutionized many of the guiding assumptions embedded in the "sacred" stories and text of his people.

DOUBTING VIOLENCE

Violence is the dominant religion in the world today. Walter Wink says violence "is the ethos of our times" and the "spirituality of the modern world." Violence is "accorded the status of a religion, demanding from its devotees an absolute obedience to death." Wink says the "roots of this devotion to violence are deep" and that violence "and not Christianity, is the real religion of America."[5] As bold as these statements are, they dramatically understate the problem. Violence today is God, the one and only functional God at the heart of most ideologies, whether capitalist, Marxist, anarchist, revolutionary, reactionary, or religious. In the secular world, superior violence is God because violence is presumed to be the only and ultimate means to security or victory or revenge.

Violence is at the heart of monotheistic faith. Proclaiming God Almighty and restricting God to One whose power is understood as superior violence means that in monotheistic religion *violence is God because violence saves God* in the sense of establishing and maintaining God's credibility. The tragic legacy of violent God and violent religion rooted in "sacred" text is not only that religion inevitably, if unconsciously, is reduced to violence. It is also our inability to see or embrace the reality and potential of nonviolent power. Judaism, Christianity, and Islam will continue to contribute to the destruction of the world unless and until each challenges violence in "sacred" texts, and until each affirms nonviolent power, including the nonviolent power of God.

Active nonviolence is an effective means to confront evil, resist injustice, defend territory, thwart enemies, and establish peace. The theory of power at the heart of the Bible and Quran is that power is based on superior, punishing, coercive violence. It is featured centrally in the bastions of male dominance today, including political, economic, military, and religious institutions. Nonviolent theory and practice are based on an alternative theory of power in which "the exercise of power depends on the consent of the ruled who, by withdrawing that consent, can control and even destroy the power of their opponent. In other words," Gene Sharp writes, "nonviolent action is a technique used to control, combat, and destroy the opponent's power by nonviolent means of wielding power."[6]

It is well beyond the scope of this book to present the impressive history of successful nonviolent movements and discuss fully the dynamics and methods of nonviolent resistance and nonviolent social change.[7] I limit myself to three observations about nonviolent power:

First, active nonviolence is an effective means of resisting evil and building greater justice. The Gandhian Independence Movement in India; Danish resistance to Nazi occupation during World War II; the U.S. civil rights or freedom movement; overthrow of dictators in Iran, the Philippines, and countries in Eastern Europe; labor movement gains; and antiwar protests—these are but some of many nonviolent success stories. Gene Sharp catalogues hundreds of successful nonviolent movements in history, describes 198 methods of nonviolent action, and details the dynamics and nuts and bolts of effective nonviolent organizing.[8]

Second, although active nonviolence has been, is, and can be effective, it needs a much broader constituency. Sharp details remarkable nonviolent success stories, but he laments how little attention is paid to the power and effectiveness of nonviolence or to enhancing its potential: "Although much effort has gone into increasing the efficiency of violent conflict, no comparable efforts have yet gone into making nonviolent action more effective and hence more likely to be substituted for violence."[9]

In all parts of the world, there are many peoples and groups, both religious and secular, who work to counter violence.[10] Nonviolent efforts to establish justice, build peace, resolve conflicts, and achieve reconciliation, however, are dwarfed by the dollars, training, weapons, and organized violence of nation states or those engaged in violent conflict with or within them. Congressman Dennis Kucinich of Ohio has a proposal to create a U.S. Department of Peace:

> The Department of Peace would focus on nonmilitary peaceful conflict resolutions, prevention of violence, and will promote justice and democratic principles to expand human rights. A peace Academy, similar to the five military service academies, would be created, [and] its graduates dispatched to troubled areas around the globe to promote nonviolent dispute resolutions.[11]

This and similar efforts hold great possibility but languish for want of an organized voice for nonviolence and peacemaking, including a "Proposal for a Global Nonviolent Peace Force" and the "Every Church a Peace Church" network. The Nonviolent Peace Force "is a trained international civilian nonviolent peace force . . . [that] works at the invitation of local groups to protect human rights and prevent death and destruction, thus creating the space for local groups to struggle nonviolently, enter into dialogue, and seek peaceful resolution."[12] The "Every Church a Peace Church" network is founded on the simple idea that Christians should pay attention to Jesus. "The church could turn the world toward peace if every church lived and taught as Jesus lived and taught."[13]

People of faith, as the "Decalogue of Assisi for Peace" (quoted above) makes clear, should be a logical constituency to live and advocate for these and other effective nonviolent programs, initiatives, training, and action. Only a tiny minority of believers, however, reject violence and also work passionately for nonviolent social change. I believe a fundamental reason why most Jews, Christians, and Muslims reject nonviolence in favor of militarization is that they embrace the God of superior violence named above. They internalize, rather than confront and reject, the violence-of-God traditions at the heart of the Bible and the Quran.

Third, I lift up two examples of powerful nonviolent action with particular relevance to the issue of religion, violence, and "sacred" text. They are that of Mohandas K. Gandhi and his Muslim follower and friend Badshah Khan. Gandhi, perhaps the most effective nonviolent strategist in history, challenged the religious foundations of violence. The Hindu tradition gave high status to a warrior caste, and it justified and required warfare and violence in its "sacred" text (the *Bhagavad Gita*). Gandhi built his concept of active nonviolence or *satyagraha* (truth-force) on the Hindu concept of *ahimsa* (no harm to living things) and the integrity of his own experience. Although the *Gita* encouraged war, Gandhi reinterpreted it to be a spiritual message requiring human beings to struggle against the violence within in order nonviolently to transform the world without. He also pointed out that the whole of the *Mahabharata* (the *Gita* was part of this larger work) revealed the futility of violence.

Gandhi's nonviolent practices were at the heart of a successful independence movement, but his religious ideas were challenged. He responded to criticism of his reinterpretation of "sacred" text by affirming his *lived experience* of the *Gita*. "I have something far more powerful than argument, namely, experience, . . . an effort to enforce the meaning in my own conduct for an unbroken period of forty years." Gandhi also said that it "is a misuse of our intellectual energy and a waste of time to go on reading what we cannot put into practice."[14] In other words, Gandhi believed that it was absurd and destructive to cling to interpretations of "sacred" texts that justify violence when the world itself, including the world of his own experience, revealed both the futility of violence and the power of nonviolence.

Evil, according to Gandhi, was always to be actively resisted. Gandhi embraced nonviolence but he preferred violent resistance to indifference or accommodation. "Nonviolence in its dynamic condition means conscious suffering. It does not mean meek submission to the will of the evildoer," Gandhi said, "but it means the pitting of one's whole soul against the will of the tyrant."[15] Gandhi concluded that active nonviolence was more effective than violence in resisting evil, working for justice, and building peace, and that nonviolence also best reflected the will and nature of God.

Badshah Khan, a follower of Gandhi, led the independence struggle against the British in the North West Frontier of India. Khan is known as the "greatest nonviolent soldier of Islam" and "one of the greatest nationalist leaders who claimed the loyalty of thousands of nonviolent Pathans."[16] Khan's movement offers hope that a powerful nonviolent stream within Islam could develop as an effective response to present injustices. His example of principled and effective nonviolence suggests an alternative to the futile spiral of violence that fractures many Islamic countries today and that characterizes U.S. state-sponsored terror and also terrorism directed at the United States.

Khan's nonviolent movement responded to the oppressive violence of illiteracy, poverty, hunger, and dysfunctional violence that characterized the life of Pathans under oppressive British rule. British policies fostered ignorance and encouraged a culture of violence, vendetta, and revenge. "The history of my people is full of victories and tales of heroism," Khan said, "but there are drawbacks, too. Internal feuds and personal jealousies have always snatched away the gains achieved through vast sacrifices."[17] We not only "failed to serve our fellow beings," Khan said, "we fought with them instead."[18] The British ruled because violent divisions prevented understanding and unified action. Khan told his people:

> Fifty percent of the children in our country are ill. The hospitals are meant for the English. The country is ours, the money is ours, everything belongs to us, but we are hungry and naked in it. We have not got anything to eat, no houses. He [the British] has made . . . roads because he needs them for himself. These roads were built with our money. Their roads are in London. These are our roads, but we are not allowed to walk on them. He excites the Hindus to fight the Muslims and the . . . Sikhs to fight the Muslims. Today these three are the sufferers. Who is the oppressor, and who has been sucking our blood?[19]

Khan and his followers opened schools, built latrines, organized other community development projects for social improvement, and educated and empowered women despite resistance from both the British and from traditional Muslim religious leaders. People who joined his movement took an oath to Allah: "I will serve the nation without any self-interest," "I will not take revenge," "My actions will be nonviolent," "I will make every sacrifice required of me to stay on this path," "I will serve the people without regard to their religion or faith," and "I shall use nation-made goods."[20]

Khan never directly addressed the violence-of-God traditions in the Quran. Instead, he drew on a Meccan tradition linking Muhammad to patience and suffering, grounded the nonviolent movement in Islamic texts that called patience and forgiveness courageous acts (Quran 42:43), and called refusal to retaliate an act of charity and atonement (5:45).[21] Much like Gandhi's spiritualization of violent passages in the *Gita* that transformed war-justifying texts, Badshah Khan called for and organized a nonviolent jihad among a people with a long history of dysfunctional feuding and violence. Khan said:

> I am going to give you such a weapon that the police and the army will not be able to stand against it. It is the weapon of the Prophet, but you are not aware of it. That weapon is patience and righteousness. No power on earth can stand against it. When you go back to your villages, tell your brethren that there is an army of God, and its weapon is patience. Ask your brethren to join the army of God. Endure all hardships. If you exercise patience, victory will be yours.[22]

When people compared him to Gandhi, Khan responded: "I am not fit for the praise you have showered on me. The praise *is due to the nonviolent method,* which has changed the nature of our people."[23] "Nonviolence was accepted," Sarfaraz Nazim says, "because, even though it was incompatible with being a Pathan, it was compatible with Islam. It was accepted by the people as a nonviolent *jihad.*"[24] Promises of paradise that had encouraged people to fight and die in violent struggles against enemies were called on to give courage to people engaged in risky nonviolent witness and action.[25] The "crux of Badshah Khan's success," said another follower, "was that he had creatively *used* the message of Islam."[26] Kahn's recognition of the futility of violence; his use of selective texts from the Quran to urge patience, courage, forgiveness, and nonretaliation; his programs to address pressing social needs; and his call for a nonviolent *jihad*—these all offer possibilities that Muslims may embrace radical nonviolence even though violence is featured centrally within their "sacred" text.

JESUS AND DOUBT

Elsewhere I have written extensively about the radical nonviolence of Jesus and his clash with the violence-of-God traditions in the Hebrew Scriptures and the Christian New Testament.[27] Here I lift up the "doubting Jesus" for two reasons. First, I want to bolster my claim that doubt is a good thing. We desperately need to doubt the violence-of-God traditions at the heart of the Bible and the Quran. If Jesus doubted, then so can we.

Second, I want to contrast Jesus with the violence and service to empire carried out in his name. Christians who embrace violence and uncritically endorse militaristic policies of the United States betray Jesus. "The crux of the extent to which Christians should fulfill their responsibilities as provisional citizens of various localities," writes Lee Griffith, "came with two defining issues: whether Christians could honor the divinity of the emperor, and whether Christians could wield weapons of war. 'No' was the resounding answer on both counts during the first three centuries of church history."[28]

Jesus was a radical Jew who doubted and challenged many of the assumptions of the Hebrew Scriptures and many of the popular ideas held with sure conviction by his contemporaries. Below I create an informal dialogue between "doubting Jesus" and his tradition:

- Our "sacred" text claims that sufficient rain is a conditional blessing. Obey God, and it will rain and the harvest will be good; disobey God and experience drought (Lev 26:4) or flood (Gen 6–7). In these words you hear that God is punishing and vindictive and withholds even the rain and sunshine necessary for good harvests. But I say to you, based on my experience, that God isn't like that. God "makes his sun rise on the evil and on the good, and sends rain on the righteous and on the unrighteous" (Matt 5:45).

- Our "sacred" text claims that God orders us to murder "all who curse father or mother" (Lev 20:1–2a, 9) and to stone to death rebellious sons (Deut 20:18–21). In these words you hear that God's violence shores up abusive patriarchal power. But I say to you, based on my experience, that God isn't like that. God wants us to challenge oppressive power wherever we see it, including within families, because abusive power prevents us from building justice and becoming the family of God (Luke 12:51–53; Mark 3:31–35).

- Our "sacred" text and our religious contemporaries say that those who break Sabbath regulations threaten to bring God's wrath on the nation and should be killed (Num 15:32–36; Mark 3:6). In these words you hear that God is violent and punishing, and that God desires holiness more than God values human life. But I say to you, based on my experience, that God is not like that. The Sabbath is a gift from a gracious God and not a burden (Mark 2:27), and civil disobedience is often a requirement of faith (Mark 3:1–6).

- Our "sacred" text says God is God because of superior violence (Deut 4:34–35; Exod 15:11–12, 16a), and that salvation means defeat of enemies (Exod 15:1–3a, 4a; Ps 18:45–48). But I say to you, based on my experience, that those who use violence perish by violence (Matt 26:52). How stupid we are to cling to the false promises of redemptive violence. It is understandable that we hate the injustices that force us from our land and that we are tempted to hate our oppressors. They reduce us to the status of near slaves, and for the benefit of others, we work land we once owned.

Some of us may even want to kill the owner's son, but "what then will the owner of the vineyard do? He will come and destroy" us and lease the vineyard to others (Mark 12:1–9). Resisting injustice by using violent means only feeds a spiral of violence. Oppressors want us to resist violently because it gives them the excuse they need to crush us. There are nonviolent strategies to deal with injustice (Matt 5:38–42), but we hold onto the false promises of our "sacred" text, deny history, and wait for fulfillment of Isaiah's illusionary promises of a glorious reversal or John the Baptist's claim that the apocalyptic end is imminent.

- Our "sacred" text promises that we will be recipients of God's preferred violence. Kings and queens who oppress us will soon be shamed. With "their faces to the ground they shall bow down" to us and they will "lick the dust" from our feet (Isa 49:23). Nations will bring us their wealth, and those who will not serve us "shall be utterly laid waste" (Isa 60: 11–12). When we tire of these unmet prophecies, we despair of history altogether and await the punishing, vindicating, apocalyptic violence of God (Matt 3:10, 12). But I say to you, based on my experience of God and history, that these are nothing but wild and dangerous fantasies. If you want to experience the realm of God, then reject messianic and apocalyptic violence and instead plant a tiny mustard seed (Mark 4:30–32). Do not think that because I reject violent images of God's power and lofty metaphors like the cedars of Lebanon that I reject God's power altogether. A mustard seed is radical, small, and subversive. Mustard plants grow where they are not wanted. Invitational power is different than coercive power, but nonetheless it is powerful. If you want to see God's realm take root in the world, then join with others and be communities of subversive weeds. Stop looking at the world through the lens of scarcity, and embrace and live according to the abundance of God (Matt 6:25–30; Luke 14:15–24; Matt 6:11; 5:42).

- Our "sacred" text says that God's power is violent and coercive, and that God's realm will be imposed by violence. But I say to you, based on my experience, that God is not going to send a Messiah to save us (Matt 18:23–35), and your apocalyptic expectations are illusionary. I tell parables that expose the oppressive system because we need to understand the system in order to change it.[29] God is not out there in the sky, and the realm of God is not far away or consigned to the Hereafter. God is the Spirit at the heart of life, inviting us to new life, and the realm is right here in our midst (Luke 17:20–21).
- Our "sacred" text and many of our friends urge us to hate enemies because they are also understood to be the enemies of God. But I tell you, based on my experience, that we should love our enemies and pray for our persecutors because only then can we break the spiral of violence. Loving enemies best reflects what God is like (Matt 5:43–45).
- Our "sacred" text and all of our expectations say that salvation is the crushing defeat of enemies. But I say to you, based on my experience, that salvation is healing and restoring to real community those who are oppressed and excluded (Mark 3:1–6). We are taught to hate Samaritans and others over petty differences, yet God isn't tribal or exclusive but welcoming. Because you were certain Samaritans could not be good, I told you a parable about a Good Samaritan helping a Jew who was beaten, left for dead, and ignored by other Jews. We love enemies because that is God's desire and, who knows, our enemies may be important to our own salvation (Luke 10:30–37).

It might be tempting to conclude, based on the "doubting Jesus," that the God of the Hebrew Scriptures is violent and punishing, and the God of the New Testament is nonviolent and loving. It would be more accurate to say that Jesus' God is nonviolent, and that the God of the Bible—in both the Hebrew Scriptures and Christian New Testament—is violent.

I believe that Christianity is almost completely severed from the radical Jesus glimpsed above. Most Christians, including those who live in the United States, have rejected Jesus, nonviolent power, and a nonviolent God while adopting superior violence as Lord and Savior. The Gospel writers, like Christianity itself, have betrayed Jesus in many ways. They interpret Jesus through images of God that Jesus himself rejected. They view Jesus as an atoning sacrifice that appeases a punishing deity, and they position the nonviolent Jesus, whom they choose to ignore, as the apocalyptic "Son of Man," who will return soon to judge and punish the world.

The survival of the world as we know it depends on our willingness to revision divine and human power. This depends on our willingness to challenge the violence-of-God traditions in the Bible and the Quran. Like Gandhi, who was inspired by the nonviolence of Jesus, we must allow Jesus' doubts to inspire our own as we question the authority of "sacred" texts that legitimate violence.

CONCLUSION

The violence-of-God traditions at the heart of the Bible and the Quran have invaded our own hearts. By sanctioning violence in "sacred" texts and in reference to them, we invariably progress along a treacherous pathway. God is powerful and proves to be God through superior violence. The God of superior violence justifies human violence in the name of God and in pursuit of God's objectives that with frightening regularity mirror our own objectives. In the end, violence replaces or becomes God. Violence is widely embraced because it is embedded and sanctified in "sacred" texts and because its use seems logical in a violent world. There is a compelling counter-logic embraced by Jesus, Dorothy Day, Gandhi, Badshah Khan, and many others, including Thich Nhat Hanh, who offers the following precepts for living in his book *Being Peace:*

- Do not be idolatrous about or bound to any doctrine, theory, or ideology.
- Do not think that the knowledge you presently possess is changeless, absolute truth.
- Do not force others, including children, by any means whatsoever, to adopt your views, whether by authority, threat, money, propaganda, or even education.
- Do not avoid contact with suffering or close your eyes before suffering.
- Do not accumulate wealth while millions are hungry. . . . Possess nothing that should belong to others.
- Do not maintain anger or hatred.
- Do not lose yourself in dispersion and in your surroundings. Learn to . . . practice mindfulness.
- Do not utter words that can create discord and cause the community to break. Make every effort to reconcile and resolve all conflicts, however small.
- Do not say untruthful things for the sake of personal interest or to impress people. . . . Always speak truthfully and constructively. Have the courage to speak out about situations of injustice, even when doing so may threaten your own safety. A religious community should . . . take a clear stand against oppression and injustice.
- Do not live with a vocation that is harmful to human[s] and nature. Do not invest in companies that deprive others of their chance to life. Select a vocation which helps realize your ideal of compassion.
- Do not kill. Do not let others kill. Find whatever [nonviolent] means possible to protect life and prevent war.
- Do not mistreat your body. . . . Be fully aware of the responsibility of bringing new lives into the world.[30]

Openness to the Spirit of truth and nonviolence reflected in these precepts offers a creative alternative to the rigid violence-of-God traditions embedded in the "sacred" texts of Jews, Christians, and Muslims. The logic behind an alternative view of power is captured in words I have hanging on my office door, from Bertha von Suttner, who inspired the Nobel Peace Prize and was one of its first recipients: "Only a fool would try to remove an ink spot with more ink, or an oil spot with oil; how can anyone believe that blood stains can be removed by shedding more blood?"

It is foolish to grant authority to the violence-of-God traditions at the heart of the Bible and the Quran. It is time to learn from our enemies, run with our doubts, and embrace the power of nonviolence. The world clamors for a constituency of nonviolent peacemakers willing to dedicate their lives to building a world of compassion and justice. It remains to be seen whether Jews, Christians, and Muslims can heed the call and overcome violence legitimated by our "sacred" texts. If we reject violence and re-envision human and divine power, then a joyous cry will be heard throughout the earth: "Thanks be to God."

NOTES

1. Eknath Easwaran, *A Man to Match His Mountains: Badshah Khan, Nonviolent Soldier of Islam* (Berkeley, Calif.: The Blue Mountain Center of Meditation, 1984), 11–12.

2. See Homer A. Jack, ed., *The Gandhi Reader* (New York: Grove Press, 1956).

3. Ivone Gebara, *Longing for Running Water: Ecofeminism and Liberation* (Minneapolis: Augsburg Fortress, 1999), 101.

4. All quotes and references to the Day of Prayer for Peace are online, www.vatican.va/special/assisi_20020124_en.html.

5. Walter Wink, *Engaging the Powers: Discernment and Resistance in a World of Domination* (Minneapolis: Fortress, 1992), 13.

6. Gene Sharp, *The Politics of Nonviolent Action* (Extending Horizons Books; Boston: Porter Sargent Publishers, 1973), 4, in Part 1.

7. See some of the references listed below.

8. See Sharp, *The Politics of Nonviolent Action,* "Part 1: Power and Struggle," "Part 2: The Methods of Nonviolent Action," and "Part 3: The Dynamics of Nonviolent Action."

9. Sharp, *The Politics of Nonviolent Action,* 4, in Part 1.

10. See, for example, Elise Boulding, *Cultures of Peace: The Hidden Side of History* (Syracuse: Syracuse University Press, 2000); George Lakey, *Powerful Peacemaking: A Strategy for a Living Revolution* (Philadelphia: New Society Publishers, 1987); John Paul Lederach, *Preparing for Peace: Conflict Transformation across Cultures* (Syracuse: Syracuse University Press, 1995).

11. For information, see online www.thespiritoffreedom.com/deptofpeace.html.

12. For information, see online www.nonviolentpeaceforce.org.

13. For information, see online www.ecapc.org.

14. This quote is from a Justice and Peace Studies textbook used at the University of St. Thomas in St. Paul, Minnesota: *How Could You Think Such a Thing: Class Notes for THEO 305,* written by my colleague in Justice and Peace Studies, Rev. David Whitten Smith. He can be reached at the university, where the book is available for purchase.

15. Quoted in Easwaran, *A Man to Match His Mountains,* 80.

16. Quoted in Mukulika Banerjee, *The Pathan Unarmed* (Santa Fe, N.M.: School of American Research Press, 2000), 1.

17. Easwaran, *A Man to Match His Mountains,* 35.

18. Ibid., 56.

19. Ibid., 60.

20. Ibid., 74.

21. Ibid., 147.

22. Ibid., 117.

23. Ibid., 131, emphasis added.

24. Ibid., 160.

25. Ibid., 154

26. Ibid., 160.

27. Jack Nelson-Pallmeyer, *Jesus against Christianity: Reclaiming the Missing Jesus* (Harrisburg: Trinity Press International, 2001).

28. Lee Griffith, *The War on Terrorism and the Terror of God* (Grand Rapids: Eerdmans, 2002), 24.

29. William R. Herzog II, *Parables as Subversive Speech: Jesus as Pedagogue of the Oppressed* (Louisville: Westminster John Knox, 1994).

30. Thich Nhat Hanh, *Being Peace* (ed. Arnold Koller; Berkeley, Calif.: Parallax Press, 1987), 89–100.

Index